WOMAN,
TAKE OFF YOUR CAPE!
STOP SAVING THE DAY AND START SAVING YOUR HEALTH

Dr. Candace McMillon-Dantley

Well Power
PUBLISHING

The stories in this book are inspired by the personal experiences and events of the author. Fictional characters, places, and products were created to entertain and educate readers while portraying the thoughts, real -life experiences and perceptions of the author. The content of this book is for informational purposes only and is not intended to diagnose, treat, cure, or prevent any condition or disease. Reading this book does not establish a doctor-patient relationship.

This book is not intended as a substitute for consultation with a licensed practitioner. Consult with your own physician or healthcare specialist regarding the suggestions and recommendations made in this book.
The use of this book implies your acceptance of this disclaimer. The publisher and the author are providing this book and its contents on an "as is" basis and make no representation or warranties of any kind with respect to this book or its contents. The publisher and author disclaim all such representations and warranties, including but not limited to warranties of healthcare for a particular purpose. In addition, the publisher and the author assume no responsibility for errors, inaccuracies, omissions, or any other inconsistencies herein.

Paperback ISBN: 978-1-73525-830-0
Library of Congress Control Number: 2020911377
Copyright © 2020 Dr. Candace McMillon-Dantley
Photography by Andrew Archer/CIK Creative Solutions
Published by WellPower Publishing, Quincy, FL

Printed in the United States of America
2020

SPECIAL SALES
Special quantity discounts may be available when purchased in bulk by corporations, organizations, and special interest groups. For information, please email wellpowerpublishing@gmail.com.

*To my beautiful, amazingly, intelligent daughter Cadence:
My prayer is that you grow into a woman that loves herself
without limits.*

CONTENTS

WOMAN,

TAKE OFF YOUR CAPE!

STOP SAVING THE DAY AND START SAVING YOUR HEALTH

1 The Cape

I almost killed myself. Not just once - at least twice a week. Nobody saw it though…even though I was standing in plain sight when it happened. What they *did* see was me standing there with a patient chart in hand and a bright smile asking, "What brings you in today?" Of course, no one saw me suffering almost to point of death. Why? Why couldn't they see? - It was the cape I was wearing.

That cape made me look happy when I was sad, strong when I was weak, healthy when I was sick, and alive when I wanted to die.

I *wanted* to take it off, but I knew if I did, I would disappoint everyone. If I took off that cape, I wouldn't be the "hero" who returned to her hometown to start a chiropractic office at twenty-six years young.

If I took off that cape, I wouldn't look *strong, smart,* and *perfect* like I did when I was the high school valedictorian. I know you're wondering, "What kind of cape can hide the fact that someone is dying?

Well, I'm not talking about the cute, mustard-colored cape on the front of this cover. I'm talking about the kind that superheroes wear. That red, flowing cape that makes a superhero look powerful, hides their injuries from battle, and sends them soaring high into the clouds!

As glorious as those capes look on superheroes, they are not meant to be worn by women as an everyday accessory. But yet and still, you put on that cape. Every. Single. Day.

To the world around you, you look strong, perfect, powerful, and indestructible. If there's a family crisis, an event that needs planning, or your boss needs someone to stay late, you *whoosh* right in to save the day! – but guess what? I know your secret …

THAT CAPE IS TOO DANG HEAVY!

The truth is, that cute little cape string tied around your neck, in a neat little bow, is strangling the life out of you! I'm sorry to expose your secret, but it had to be done! If you're honest with yourself, you feel relieved that someone *finally* noticed the weight you've been carrying on your shoulders.

How do you plan to keep this up? *Saving* everyone else's day while *suffering* through your own? You have two options:

Option One: You can keep playing the superhero - *whooshing* around, to and fro, pretending that your body never aches or your heart never bleeds (I've tried this one - it doesn't work.).

Option Two: You can TAKE. OFF. YOUR. CAPE!

One year ago, I decided to take off my cape and save *me*. I released the weight of always saying "YES!", when I needed to say "NO." I stopped killing myself just so I could live for what other people wanted me to be in *their* lives. I stopped listening to everyone's opinion about *my* life and started listening to God instead. I decided to be who *I* needed to be for *me*.

For years, I cheerfully suffered through the exhaustion of trying not to disappoint others. Behind the scenes I lived in the pits of failure, weakness, and depression. I gave my all to be the perfect mom, the world's greatest wife, the most supportive family member, and the best doctor- but I didn't give anything to myself.

It wasn't easy to take off a cape that seemingly so many people depended on me to wear. However, God gave me the tools in this book that allowed me to toss the weight and live my true passion and purpose! Today, I'm *healthier*, *happier*, and *stronger* in my mind, body, and spirit - It feels amazing!

After you read this book, I hope that your eyes are opened to what "cape-wearing" has robbed you of. I hope that you choose to reclaim your physical, mental, and spiritual health. Why? Because you deserve the same "on top of the world" feeling that I have!

As you untie your cape strings, and watch your cape fall to the ground, I hope you embrace the lightness and brightness that your life has to offer YOU!

But first, you must look in the mirror and *truly* see yourself - without the cape. Think of this book as your mirror. While reading this book, you will see your reflection through the lives of everyday women who wear capes, just like you.

Through their stories, you will discover how easily "cape-wearing" exposes your body, mind, and spirit to health conditions that affect women the most. You may even realize that not only have you been wearing one cape, but you've been wearing two or three at the same time.

As a doctor, I will reveal to you the health conditions, risks, signs, and symptoms associated with "cape-wearing". As a wife, mother, daughter, sister, and friend, I will encourage you on this journey of self-discovery and empowerment.

I will gift to you the tools that shaped my transformation into a woman who is free from the weight of the cape! I think we can both agree - you've worn the cape long enough! It's time to take off your cape and live your healthiest life – mind, body, and spirit! If you don't, *who will save you?*

2 Heart and Soul

"❝LET'S GO TRENT!❞", I hated yelling up the stairs *every* single morning. It was a part of the routine now since his dad wasn't here.

"OK MA! ONE SECOND... I'M COMING!", Trent yelled from the upstairs bathroom.

As I poured the hazelnut creamer, his footsteps sounded like a stampede hurrying across the hall – probably looking for his gym bag again. His room looked like a hot-pig-pen-mess! He was always looking for something!

I grabbed my canister and headed towards the front door. Trent made a quick leap over the last three steps and was standing in the foyer. He looked at me like a puppy who got caught chewing a leather shoe, cute and guilty.

I looked up towards his dark chocolate eyes and perfectly sponged coils and said,

"About time you came down Mr. America!"

"How in the world can it take so long to put on a T-shirt and baller shorts?!"

"Ma, you know, it's a process to have this much swagga. Gotta be fresh for the ladies - know what I'm sayin'?" He flashed his braces and licked his lips like he was LL Cool J.

I cut him a sharp side-eye as I punched in the alarm code and said, "Boy please! *Swagga* out of this door before you make us late! You'll be fresh alright — fresh out of luck!

He threw his hand over his mouth and snickered as if I couldn't hear him. Since the divorce, I drove Trent to Pine Grove Middle School every morning.

It was a pain in the butt getting him out of the house on time, but I didn't mind spending extra time with him on the way to school. Before I knew it, I was cruising around the pavement of the parent drop off circle.

"Have an awesome day Pastor T.W. Jakes!", I said cheerfully.

"Ma, can you *please* stop calling me that – like for real, for real?", he begged as I pressed the button to unlock the door.

"I can't make you any promises, but I'll try *real* hard," I shrugged my shoulders and smiled.

Trent was the only four-year-old we knew that begged to wear his church suit to Pre-K so, Pastor T.W. (short for Trenton Wallace) Jakes seemed like a perfect fit back then - he was so cute!

"See you later Super Mom," he said in the baritone voice he had gotten over the summer.

I watched Trent walk across the grass onto the sidewalk - he's really growing up! I thank God Trent is such a good child

(Even though he got on my *last* nerves some days and made me rethink this whole "motherhood" thing).

I was beyond grateful that he was never in trouble and did well in school. I cranked up the music and sang along to one of my "Girl-You-Can-Do-Anything" anthems. Today was gonna be a good one! - I could just feel it!

The Soul Pot

There was a short lady with long strands of salt and pepper waiting at the counter as soon as I set foot in the door. My eyes smiled at her as I introduced myself.

"I'm Sandra, how may I help you today?" She smiled brightly and she said,

"I'm Mrs. Sanders. We're havin' our annual brunch for Rev. Fields – you know down at New Zion Baptist?" – I nodded a quick yes.

"And we want you to cater it for us - everybody just *loves* your cooking!"

"I would be honored to cater it! What'd you have in mind?"

She unfolded a crumpled sheet of paper and started reading off,

"Biscuits, bacon – not that lil' thin bacon but the thick kind – , scrambled eggs…"

As soon as she said "*bacon"* my mind traveled back into time. Every morning, the aroma and sizzle of thick cut bacon strips on a cast iron skillet filled the small, pale yellow painted house where I grew up.

7

I pointed to the price list and said,

"This option will feed one hundred people. It includes all the foods you want, orange juice, coffee, and paper goods."

"This'll be ready by next Saturday?", she asked with a look of concern.

"Yes Mrs. Sanders! I'll be there with food so good it'll make you want to slap yo' mama, yo' daddy, *and* Rev Fields too!"

She burst into a high- pitched squeal and slapped her knee, "I'm looking forward to it!"

I couldn't believe all the new catering orders that were coming through the restaurant! - through *my* restaurant! I don't like to toot my own horn, but *Sandy's Soul Pot*, was THEE BEST spot, for soul-food cooking on this side of heaven!

We have homemade peach cobbler, baked mac and cheese, chicken and dumplings, fried green tomatoes - you name it! Customers like Mrs. Sanders made me proud of my accomplishments!

Last month, the Chamber awarded us with the title, "Lowndes County's #1 Restaurant" and we received recognition for our most popular dish, Granny's Chicken and Waffles.

People who really know me aren't surprised by the success of my restaurant – I've been cooking since I was four years old! My skinny lil' legs would climb on that old, wooden crate and stand alongside my grandmother.

I would gaze at her mixing cornbread batter, coating chicken thighs with flour for frying, and cutting heaps of collard greens to cook with smoked ham hocks… Mmm, mmm!

WOMAN TAKE OFF YOUR CAPE

Every Sunday afternoon, I would spin and twirl in my daisy covered apron and imagine I was a chef. *Clink, clank, clink, clank* filled the kitchen as I rummaged through the cabinets – gathering up pots and pans, large and small. I loved cooking for my family and my family loved me cooking for them!

Being that I'm the eldest of five, I always helped Momma and Daddy take care of the others. I can still hear myself humming and singing *Amazing Grace* as I poured my heart and soul into batches of flaky, homemade biscuits and 3-layered chocolate cakes.

"TIME TO EAT!",

I'd call out to my brothers and sisters. It's funny how they'd all run to the table as if they were chasing down a school bus that left them.

"Sandy, you put your foot in these yams!", Daddy would say.

"Mmm, Mmm Sandy! Deeee-licious!" my brother would say as he rubbed his belly.

My mom would smile in approval as she dipped her biscuit into the brown gravy. Our tiny, little dining room was filled with smacking lips, contagious laughter, and tight bellies after we'd all stuffed ourselves full - the good ole' days!

The business side of things keep me busy, but not too busy to throw on my black apron and make the pots sing! A simple thing like watching buttermilk biscuits rise in the oven sparked that magic I felt as a child.

Soul-ly Responsible

Knock ..knock. "It's open, come in!", I answered.

Faith strolled in with a list longer than a network movie with commercials.

"Good morning Boss Lady, just here to remind you how busy you are today – she placed a To-Do List on the corner of the desk.

"Newspaper ad, quotes for the walk-in freezer, new dessert on the menu, *and* you have to pick Trent up from practice."

"My God, you keep this boss busy!", I said while jokingly shaking my head as I signed the food order form in front of me.

"I reckon that's why you hired me Boss Lady – be back in one hour to make sure you stay on task!", I could hear her smiling as she closed the door behind her.

She wasn't *exactly* right – I *hired* her to take some of the busy work off my plate. She wasn't doing that though – I wouldn't let her!

"Looking forward to it," I hollered through the office door.

I know I'm just plain ol' crazy for not letting her do what I'm paying her to do! She's more than capable of getting the job done, but this restaurant is *my* baby!

The thought of letting someone else make decisions makes me nervous and uneasy – I'd rather do it myself! Truth be told, I'm struggling to get it all done. Now, I have all this extra stuff with Trent.

Denzel was the one that picked him up, dropped him off, and went to practices – that was all on me now. Both of us agreed it was best for me to keep the house and raise Trent. I didn't know me keeping the house meant he would move out of town! – I got bamboozled!

I thought he would stay nearby for Trent, but nooo! He *conveniently* took a job outside of Atlanta *and* he didn't even tell us until his stuff was packed in boxes – the nerve!

From the outside looking in, I have it all together, but that was far from the truth! Managing a growing business, helping my parents, and raising a son in this day and age was more challenging than I ever imagined.

It had only been two years since our divorce. Don't get me wrong, after 15 years of arguing, lies, misunderstandings, and broken hearts, it was for the best. But I *did* miss havin' an extra set of hands.

"Hey Boss Lady," Faith came barging in just as I was finalizing the newspaper ad,

"Your momma wants to speak with you – she's on the phone."

"Ok, put her through the line," I replied.

It wasn't like Momma to call me during work hours. I nervously picked up the phone, "Hey Momma – everything alright?"

She responded, "Yo' daddy brought me to this hospital. I *told* him it ain't nothing wrong with me, probably just old age...either that or gas."

Lord, this lady *hated* going to the doctor – the eye doctor, the foot doctor, she hated them all! She thought that liniment and that green rubbing alcohol could cure anything!

"Ok Momma, where is Daddy?"

"He's sittin' ova there with his arms all tied across his chest and his face all balled up like he been suckin' on a lemon!"

"Momma, let me speak to Daddy please," I was trying hard to hold my peace.

"Sandy Girl!", Daddy said on the other end. I could tell he was trying to hide his frustration with Momma, too.

"Hey Daddy, what's going on with Momma?"

He answered, "Well, ya know, …"

Whenever he started with, "Well, ya know" he was about to give you a full episode.

"She been bellyaching since last week! Talm 'bout it feel like somebody poking huh feet, like a pin cushion. I said, 'Let's go to the doctor!' and she said 'That's regular for me!'"

"So, this mornin' I pulled huh socks off and good gracious alive! Her feet looked like clown shoes! – ain't nothing *regular* 'bout that! So, I made her come get checked out!"

"You did the right thing Daddy. What did the doctors say?"

"Well ya know, they say they wanna run some tests to check for sugar and some other stuff," he said with uncertainty.

WOMAN, TAKE OFF YOUR CAPE

"Ok Daddy, I'll be there with food and some clothes as soon as I can – and don't worry, Momma will be fine."

He replied, "I'll see ya lata Sandy Girl."

Out of the Williams Gang, I was the only one that stuck around Valdosta. My parents still lived in that same pale, yellow painted house on King Lane. Since they're getting up in age, I make it my business to run errands for them and go with them to doctor's appointments.

More times than I can count, I tried persuading them to move into my four – bedroom house with me and Trent. That way, I could help Daddy "manage" Momma and her charades a little better.

There was no way they would ever leave that old house though – I can't say I blame them either. There were so many memories of love, laughter, and family shared between those walls. It's hard to leave something like that behind.

Judging by the line of cars on Patterson street, it was already five o'clock. I wrapped up the last of my To Do List and straightened up my desk.

"Faith, I'm heading out for the day," I said as I gathered my pocketbook and coffee cannister.

"Alright Boss Lady. The receipts and totals for today will be on your desk first thing tomorrow…Don't forget to pick up Trent!" she yelled just as I put my hand on the door handle.

Oh Lord, I almost forgot to pick up my own child! – for the third time this week! Thank God, somebody has a working brain around here!

"Thanks, Faith!" I yelled back trying to cover up my embarrassment.

Doing everything on your own and trying to remember it all is the one thing I hate about being divorced. Somedays, I feel like I'm completely failing Trent.

I wanna be the loud-mouthed basketball mom holding the glittery sign yelling, "That's my baby!" after every shot – even the airballs. Going to a few of the games wasn't enough, but at least, I cooked three days a week.

Just like my dad and brothers, Trent loves my cooking! My southern fried chicken, with a side of white rice drizzled with brown gravy, and a super-sized bowl of banana pudding is his favorite meal.

Tonight, he was going to have to settle for eating *Burger Hut* with his grandparents in a hospital room – Lord, please don't let us be here all night!

Ab-Soul-lutely Nothing

"How's your momma doing? – Is she ok?", Faith asked while handing me a hot cup of expresso.

"Thanks…after last night, I'm gonna need a second cup of this. Momma took off the blood pressure cuff and was about to take out her IV until I grabbed her hand! All because the doctors wanted her to stay another night!"

"For real?", Faith asked with her eyebrows raised.

"For real! Long story short, they let her go home at three in the morning. I think I saw one of the nurses smiling when she left – I can't blame her!"

Faith looked at me with wide eyes – we tried to hold it in,

"Ha HAAA, Lord HAMERCYYY!!", we both just about laughed ourselves sick!

"Whew! I have to laugh to keep from crying with that lady! Anyway, I'm about to schedule a follow-up for Momma. Then, I'll meet with the kitchen staff."

"Alright, I'll have everything ready to go at nine-thirty," Faith said with assurance and headed towards the office door.

I was really worried about Momma. Last night, the doctor said she has diabetes. I don't really know much about diabetes, but I know it can kill you... Daddy needs my help more than ever.

After the meeting and taking three catering orders. I went over the "To Do" List for my house... I *really* need to fold up that basket of laundry – we been digging through it all week! Trying to find matching socks in that mess was enough to make you lose your mind!

"What you got planned for the weekend Boss Lady?", Faith asked with the daily receipts in hand.

"After I cater that family reunion, just catch up on housework, and create some new recipes."

"That's it?, she asked with disappointment.

I'll probably go see that new movie with my girl Angela Basset," I said, knowing good and well I wasn't going to nobody's movies.

After the divorce, I threw myself into running my business. Outside of the restaurant, my social life was pretty much non-existent. For fifteen years, I was married to a homebody – he didn't like being around people if he didn't have to. I consumed myself with being a good wife and mother. Eventually, I lost touch with the few associates I did have.

"Oh, that'll be good Boss Lady! You definitely could use some *me time* – especially after the week you just had."

"For real! I'll see you on Monday, have a good weekend Faith!"

"You, too Boss Lady and don't –"

"I'm headed to pick him up now!", I yelled over my shoulder as I exited the back door.

Soul Mates

I cozied my plus-sized body into my plush lavender robe and propped my feet on the beige ottoman. Catering fried chicken and sides for four-hundred, hungry people had worn me slap out! I flipped to the *Chick Flick Movie Marathon*. It wasn't no Angela Bassett, but it'll do.

The weekends had a way of making me feel kinda lonely. Trent wasn't a baby anymore. He was across the street at Omar's house playing video games. When he wasn't doing that, he was playing basketball at the *YMCA* or visiting his dad.

I was happy he was growing up, but at the same time I wished he still wanted to go to the zoo or park with me. The peace and quiet of being alone was nice, but from time-to-time I

back, but *everybody* I knew had high blood pressure! None of 'em was having heart attacks though – just me!

Most mornings, when I remembered, I swallowed the pill my doctor prescribed me right before I chewed my antacids. This doesn't make sense! – How did this happen to me?

How am I going to get the catering orders done, do the purchase orders, or run the *Soul Pot*? I worked so hard to get here and now this?

3 The Boss Woman

From law firms to cupcake shops, women are running the world and owning it! More women are becoming entrepreneurs and CEOs than ever! As of 2018, there are 12.3 million businesses that are owned by women (1) - You go Boss Woman!

The Boss Woman is highly skilled at organizing, managing, and executing her vision for the success of her business(es). Not only is she the CEO of her business(es), but she is the CEO of her family as well. Very often, the Boss Women is so consumed by the "busyness" of business and life, she makes little to no time for "owning" her health.

The Boss Woman wears the Cape of Responsibility that says, "I'm obligated to take care of *everything* and *everyone* in my world." With that being said, it's not uncommon for the Boss Woman to ignore the signs and symptoms of physical, mental, or emotional illness.

Instead of giving her health the proper attention by taking a prescription or sticking to a wellness plan, she usually has more "important business" to handle.

The Boss Woman possesses excellent leadership qualities, as one would expect. Although good leadership is essential for business, sometimes it backfires on the Boss Woman. She's so accustomed to being a leader, that it can be difficult for her to recognize when to step aside and let someone else lead. In addition, others around her may not step up to the plate because they know she has it "under control". This adds unnecessary tasks that take away valuable time for self-care.

The Boss Woman can be a bit of a workaholic. If she has the choice between going to the office to squeeze in a little more work or doing something fun or relaxing, which do you think she chooses? *Ding-ding-ding!* She's going to work!

The Boss Woman often has no sense of a healthy work/life balance. Very often, there is an internal tug-of-war over choosing what's good for herself versus choosing what is good for her business. Even when she's on her sick bed, she's still thinking about the well-being of her business.

Business plays a significant part in how she and others define who she is as a person. If she isn't careful, her personal identity can be overshadowed by the title that she carries in business. It is extremely easy to lose yourself when everyone sees you as "The Hair Slayer" instead of Sylvia or "Doctor" instead of Candace.

When she shows up to the Saturday Barbeque, instead of friends and family caring to ask, "How have you been?", they ask questions like: "What kind of hair dye is good for my sensitive scalp?" or "I get a family discount...right?"

24

If the Boss Woman never unplugs from her business, she becomes overwhelmed, overworked, and underpaid (especially if she's giving everybody the hook-up). The characteristics of the Boss Women combined with The Cape of Responsibility, can open the floodgates of illness, loss of self and disappointment. Sandra's story sheds light on just how deadly this combination can be, especially when the Boss Woman isn't honest with herself about her health.

The Healthy Truth About Sandra

Just like BFFs, Sandra and soul food had a long history. From standing on the wooden crate next to her grandmother to owning a successful restaurant and catering business, food had always been an important part of her life.

Preparing soul food meals became one of her greatest outward expressions of love towards her family and her community. The food she cooked brought bright smiles to every mouth that consumed it, including hers.

Eating gave Sandra a nostalgic euphoria that brought her to the happy times she spent with her family. Soul food became her medicine for emotional pain and her reward for accomplishments. Although Sandra had been to culinary school and learned how to prepare all kinds of healthy recipes, cooking soul food was closest to her heart.

Sandra thought of herself as a healthy, voluptuous, curvy girl. She dressed herself in attractive clothing and accessories that accentuated her best physical features. Ninety-five percent of the time, she was comfortable in her own skin. However, her health statistics told a different story.

Don't get me wrong, being confident in your appearance is a great accomplishment for any woman these days. However, don't let self-confidence and a "cute shape" deceive you into thinking that you're healthy! Sandra's health history included several risk factors that she could have prevented. Instead, she ignored those things because she was too busy and most of the time, she felt and looked fine.

Sandra's failure to make her health a priority and her relationship with food put her at risk for the number one killer of women in the United States, heart disease. A few years earlier, Sandra was diagnosed with hypertension (high blood pressure) and hypercholesterolemia (high cholesterol).

Hypertension is called "The Silent Killer" for a reason! Hypertension will allow you to perform your entire day-to-day routine during the week and have a good time on the weekend. You may not even notice the subtle symptoms that your health is going downhill. Besides, a Boss Woman would never let a little headache stop the show - Right? That mindset works fine until one day while you're busy running the world, it hits you like a freight train, *BAM!* - A heart attack!

The subtle signs of uncontrolled hypertension, like headaches or changes in vision, can easily be ignored by a Boss Woman. Hypertension is a risk factor for heart disease because over time, it damages the heart and blood vessels.

Heart disease covers more than just heart attacks. It covers atherosclerosis, which may *lead* to heart attack or stroke, coronary artery disease, congenital heart disease, and congestive heart failure. These conditions affect the structures of your heart and how it works.

Some of the risk factors for heart disease are beyond our control like gender, age and genetic factors. However, we can prevent many of the risk factors like obesity, smoking and stress by making lifestyle changes.

At her last exam, Sandra measured five feet, three-inches tall and weighed one-hundred-ninety-two pounds. According to Body Mass Index (BMI) charts, Sandra is obese and at higher risk for heart disease because of her height and weight. Standard BMI charts use height and weight as a measure of whether you are at a healthy weight.

Since the 1970s, the number of adults in the obese category has increased. Recently, for women under the age of 60, the number has tapered off. A woman with a normal or healthy weight has a BMI of 18.5 to 24.9. If you are overweight, your BMI will range from 25 to 29.9 (2).

Sandra's BMI is 34, which falls into the obese category of 30 or above. Although BMI charts don't take a woman's body fat percentage or muscle mass into account, many doctors and insurance companies use them to screen your health. Along with BMI, the risk factors that are in your control to combat heart

Smoking

Type II Diabetes I

Mental Stress and Depression

Little to No Exercise

More than 1 alcoholic beverage per day

Diet high in trans and saturated fat, sugar, and salt

disease are:

27

On one hand, Sandra took her prescribed medications for hypertension and high cholesterol (when she remembered). On the other hand, she did not make any lifestyle changes through diet and exercise. Lifestyle changes are a necessity in the fight against heart disease.

4 Boss Up On Your Health!

Boss Woman, each day you put on the Cape of Responsibility to successfully execute and fulfil the needs of your career and your family. You are very familiar with leadership and taking accountability for your family and team. How can you take these "Boss Woman" traits and go from being the boss of your world to the boss of your health?

First, let's take a look at what you eat. Contrary to what our minds and stomachs tell us, we *can* control what we eat! However, I'll admit that our eating habits have a "genetic" component that's deeply rooted in family history and traditions. This has a great impact on *what* we cook, *how* we cook, and *what* we eat.

For example, Sandra's diet consisted of recipes that she learned from her grandmother. Sandra's grandmother came from a large family where money was tight, even for necessities like food. They couldn't afford to buy healthy, lean cuts of meat and fresh produce.

Sandra's grandmother learned how to cook from her mother (Sandra's great grandmother). So, when Sandra's grandmother had her own family (Sandra's mother), she cooked fatty meats fried with lard, made biscuits from processed white flour, cooked pounds of white rice and any vegetable that she could get for cheap. Salt, a trigger for hypertension, was used heavily to season food and cure meat to prevent it from spoiling.

As a Boss Woman with a successful career, Sandra had access to healthier food options. However, she still chose to cook the way her grandmother had taught her. Why? It was because this way of cooking was etched into her DNA and passed from one generation to the next.

You must un-learn what you were taught and begin making choices that lead to healthy lifestyle changes. Eating new foods may seem overwhelming and foreign, but trust me, you will find healthy foods that you love! Just give it a try!

If the thought of changing your entire diet scares you, start by making simple changes to your eating habits. Increasing your water intake or drinking one soda a day instead of three can help you maintain a healthy weight and improve blood sugar levels. Making one small change and mastering it can make a huge impact on your health.

Cutting back on fried foods can help improve your cholesterol. Being consistent with the changes to your diet can significantly reduce your risk of heart disease. Try trading cake and cookies for fresh fruit salads or dried fruit. If you struggle to get in all of your daily nutrients, taking a supplement may be a good option for you.

One secret to being successful with making healthy food choices is to avoid depriving yourself. What I mean is, if you have been thinking about brownies for the last two weeks, just ONE

SERVING of brownie will not derail your health goals. Depriving yourself can lead to you eating an entire pan of brownies or overeating other foods to kick the brownie cravings. Eliminating too many things from your diet can lead to overeating or binging on foods that are not healthy. Moderation and portion control is the key to embracing healthy eating habits for the long-term.

What kind of diet can help you avoid the biggest scare of your life? The American Heart Association recommends The DASH (Dietary Approaches to Stop Hypertension) diet to combat hypertension without the use of medication. The DASH diet also has positive effects on blood sugar for diabetics and it helps to maintain a healthy weight (3).

If you want to learn more about the DASH diet, there are several online resources. If you need help getting started, talk to a dietitian or nutritionist. In the meantime, I've created an easy way to help you remember the foods that you can eat on the DASH diet:

Dr. Candace's 5 L's to Loving Your Heart

- ♡ Low sodium, trans fat and saturated fat
- ♡ Limited sugary foods and drinks
- ♡ Less processed foods, more whole grains
- ♡ Lot's of green vegetables, moderate fruit
- ♡ Lean cuts of meat and fish

Lifestyle changes, like these along with exercising at least 30 minutes per day, make a great impact on lowering risks for heart disease.

The thought of thirty minutes of daily exercise can seem overwhelming for a Boss Woman. You may be asking yourself, "When do I have time to do something extra?" The truth is, exercising for your health doesn't have to be time consuming!

You can divide your exercise routine into two, fifteen-minute sessions or three, ten-minute sessions. The biggest secret to being consistent is to select exercises that you enjoy! Exercise shouldn't feel like a chore. What woman in her right mind wants more chores to do? Not any of the women that I know!

If you enjoy dancing, turn on some music or go to a *Zumba®* class! If you have two left feet and dancing is not your thing, go for a brisk walk, jog, sign up for classes at the gym, or hire a personal trainer. The options are endless so, excuses should be non-existent! Making small changes like taking the stairs or parking farther away from the store can add to your health. Whatever you choose, just get moving and reduce your risk for heart disease!

As a Boss Woman, you make the time for everything and everyone in your life. You tell yourself, "I'll eat better once the kids are grown or I'll start working out once things slow down at work." That way of thinking puts you at risk for heart disease and other health conditions.

To maintain good health, you must put *your health* on *your schedule*. You must put emphasis on saving your health before saving others. Remember, this is a PROCESS! Have patience with yourself. If you fall of the wagon, get back on! If you need someone to help you stay on track with your healthy eating journey, make the sacrifice to hire a nutritionist, dietician, or purchase a program that your doctor approves of. You're a Boss Woman, you can do this!

5 The Strong Don't Survive

She slid the heavy books onto the shelf as if they were contagious. "I guess it'll be between eating or studying this semester - these prices are ridiculous!", the hazel-eyed girl said.

"Tuh! No wonder everybody is going to the bookstore around the corner," she continued her rant.

"Yeah... I've heard about that place, too ... *Books and More* I think is the name," said Andrea.

"Yep! That's the one!", she said while looking over her shoulder at Andrea who was skimming through an over-sized textbook.

"I think I'm gonna give them a try, because like you said, 'A girl's gotta eat'!"

Andrea began stacking four large books onto the shelf, one by one.

"I can offer *both of you* my manager's discount *AAAND* if

you're interested, we're hiring new employees for this semester."

The gold bangles clinked together as the girl folded her arms across her fuchsia blouse.

"How much of a discount?", she asked.

"Well, I can do twenty and...."

"Let's get to *Books and More* before they close!" she said as she grabbed Andrea's hand and darted for the door.

"Ladies, ladies! I can give you my manager's *AAAND* your employee discount for thirty-five percent off! - Books and a job!... Deal?"

"Deal!", she replied as she shook the manager's hand and gave Andrea a quick wink.

That was the day Andrea met Brandy. Their personalities were like magnets, opposite yet drawn to each other. They spent many late nights in *Andros*, the campus café, gaining their "Freshmen Fifteen" with bowls of frosted cereal and pepperoni pizza.

They shared laughs and tears, talking about guys, hometown drama, and every now and then, they studied psychology. After graduation, Andrea delayed her career plans and moved back to Tallahassee to take of her dad. Her dad suffered from multiple sclerosis and could no longer drive or cook for himself.

It was no surprise when Brandy decided to take her brains, beauty, and competitive nature to the School of Law at Wake Forest University. Different cities couldn't keep them apart though. It wasn't the same as college, but every other week, they chatted on the phone for hours.

Andrea was a strong supporter for Brandy during some of her toughest days in law school. When Brandy was cramming for her final exams, Andrea would make the nine-hour drive to help her study and make sure she didn't skip meals.

Andrea couldn't wait for her shift to be over. This week had tested and tried her patience in every way possible. She had plans to kick off the weekend with a much needed *Girls' Night Out* - it was long overdue.

"Last one for today," she whispered to herself. She gathered the electronic chart and walked into the exam room.

"So, you were coughing up green stuff for two weeks before you decided to call me Mr. Wells?" asked Andrea.

"I thought a strong man like me could... ya know, tough it out," he shrugged while glancing down at his tattooed biceps."

"Mr. Wells, unfortunately the gym can't cure an infection.", Andrea replied.

His masculinity seemed to deflate with each deep breath he took as Andrea pressed her stethoscope against his back.

"A respiratory infection like this along with your asthma can make you really sick. Don't *ever* wait to call me for something like this... ok?"

His lip started to droop, like a child getting chastised in front of his friends. He nodded in agreement.

"Just be sure to take this prescription, get some rest, and you will be as good as new," she said to ease the tension.

35

Andrea watched him exit the exam room with a bruised ego and his tail tucked between his legs.

'Why do men think they can *macho* their way out of everything? ... even their deathbeds!', she thought as she exited the room.

The patients tested Andrea's patience on several occasions, but she couldn't imagine herself doing anything else. Becoming the Director of Nursing at Woodward Medical Center was her dream come true!

Andrea was always drawn to taking care of others. At USF, she roomed with a bashful girl from Ft. Pierce, Florida named Alicia. Some days, Alicia would cry as she lied in bed for hours in pain from sickle cell disease.

On days like that, Andrea brought her a warm cup of soup, crackers, and Gatorade from the campus convenient store. She would even call Student Health Services to help Alicia when she was in crisis.

Through that experience, Andrea discovered her passion for nursing. She ate, slept, and breathed nursing while earning a Master of Nursing degree from the University of North Carolina at Chapel Hill two years ago.

Andrea was ready to get the weekend started, but not before putting the finishing touches on her reports. She wanted them flawless for the Quality Assurance Committee (QAC) meeting on Monday.

An hour skipped by as fast as a terrified patient's heartbeat. Andrea hurriedly scooped up her lunch bag, black leather purse, and pranced towards the elevator. This weekend was going to be

36

one for the books! It was always a good time when she and her girls met up at their favorite spot, *The Social*.

Imagining the sounds of brass from the live band intertwined with the aroma of spicy honey wings and fine cologne fueled her anticipation. The elevator doors slid open and she scurried onto the parking deck towards the space marked "117".

Andrea swayed her hips from side-to- side inside the peanut butter leather seat as the beat of *"Poison"* thumped through the speakers.

She rolled into the driveway of their two-story, Italian fieldstone bricked home. Mike's car wasn't in the two-car garage. By this time, he and the kids, Olivia and Bryson, were probably high on pizza and games at *The Wonder Zone*.

Andrea dashed upstairs, got showered, and slipped into one of her little black dresses and a pair of red stilettos. She smeared her full lips with a matte red lipstick and wand curled her dark brown hair.

As her reflection stared back at her, she felt grateful and blessed to have a life like this - great family, great career, and great friends! Like the perfect pair of jeans, everything just fit!

Strong Bonds

Andrea spotted her girl's laser red convertible soon as she drove into the parking lot. She was probably sitting at the bar, sipping on a martini, and schooling some random dude on how Wake Forest would take the championship this year- that girl loved herself some Wake Forest!

When she stepped into the lobby area, a tall gentleman greeted her, "Welcome to *The Social*. How many are joining you this evening?"

Before she could answer, Kristin stepped into the lobby with legs as long as a mile and a black and white jumpsuit that fit like a glove.

She threw her arms around Kristin and replied, "This fine lady right here and the beautiful one at the bar in the sapphire dress."

The greeter escorted them to a dimly lit booth in the lounge area. As they slid into the booth, Kristen said,

"I'll text her and let her know where we're sitting."

"I don't think she even saw us," Andrea said.

"Girl, she was too busy running her mouth to see us! - as usual!", Kristin said as she rolled her eyes toward the ceiling.

The ladies high-fived across the table and cackled hysterically. At that moment, they could see Brandy sashaying towards them.

"Attorney "H" to the "A" to the "L" to the "L"!" Kristin shouted.

"Heeeey, sexy ladies!", Brandy smiled as bright as the sequins on her dress. "Ya'll ready for this?!"

"Now, you know we could *NEVER* be ready for you!", Kristin replied.

"And you already know it!" Brandy responded.

It was two years ago when the BFFs found themselves together again. Brandy landed a job at one of the most prestigious firms in Charlotte, Bailey and Briggs.

After one year at the firm, Brandy took a leap of faith and opened her own law office. Andrea spent countless weekends and evenings helping with bookkeeping, scheduling, marketing, or anything that Brandy needed to get her practice off the ground.

They slid around the booth table and wasted no time catching up on all the happenings at home, work, and just life in general.

"I'm so glad that my divorce is fiii-nally over! I never would've thought Keith would be an insensitive idiot in marriage *and* divorce!"

Brandy raised her hand like a kindergartner and said, "*I* thought he would!"

Kristen replied through a chuckle, "I guess we *all* kinda did, but he wasn't always like that … I'm just thankful I had my girls to help me through that nightmare."

"Andrea, you picked up my kids from after school and cried with me at four in the morning. Brandy, you hooked me up with an attorney who got me every penny I deserve! I just didn't think I would ever get to my happy place…I love ya'll for that.!"

"That's what I'm here for!", responded Andrea.

"You know we always got your back and we're down for whatever you need!", Brandy said.

"Is there anything I can get you ladies? Maybe a round of

drinks to start?", asked the waitress.

"Uhhh, let me see…", Andrea scanned the menu as if she didn't always order the same thing.

"I'll have two baskets of spicy honey wings, cheese sticks, and a round of margaritas – Can you put this on my tab?"

"Sure thing! Everything will be out shortly," the waitress said as she collected the menus.

"Andrea, you always spoil us!", said Kristin.

"It's been months since we did this and you deserve it! Let's laugh, eat, drink, and laugh some more!", said Andrea."

"Let me tell ya'll about my date with the dude from Georgia," Brandy interrupted.

"On his profile picture, he was soooo fine! So fine that I wanted to get licensed in Georgia *and* the surrounding states! Not only was he fine, but he had credentials!

"So, how did the date go?", Kristin asked.

"As soon as he stepped out of the car, I looked at his shoes, you know busted shoes equal a busted man," Brandy continued.

"Uh-huh, that should have been the first red flag with Keith!", Kristen commented.

"Yep, 'cause Keith's s shoes looked like they had two jobs - one on *his* feet and one on some other dude's feet who walked for a living – down a dirt road! I tried to tell you he wasn't gone be right!", Brandy said, causing an explosion

40

of high-pitched squeals and table slapping.

"Oh, dear Jesus I can't breathe! Girl, you are crazy!" said Andrea, as she slid down the black leather seat with her hand on her chest.

"The shoes will tell you EVER-REY thing! ... wait, wait... ya'll hear that?", asked Brandy

The entire lounge was singing and swaying to *Before I Let Go* by Frankie Beverly and Maze. They looked at each other and said, "That's our song!"

They darted towards the dance floor and danced until their stilettoes screamed.

Strong Hit

The glass, double doors swung open when Andrea scanned her badge at the employee entrance. Andrea insisted on getting an early start on Mondays.

She used the extra hour to take inventory of the nurses' supply closet and put finishing touches on her team's schedule to ensure a smooth flow. Besides, she wanted to give her patients as much time as she could during regular hours.

She filled her stainless-steel cup with coffee and vanilla creamer and headed to the nurse's station for greetings and updates. She logged into the EHR software to check her schedule.

Suddenly, she remembered today was the meeting with QAC. Andrea hit the ground running and treated eight new patients, with symptoms ranging from bad coughs to genital rashes. Then, she followed up with Mr. Wells to make sure he was improving and following her instructions.

And just like that, her morning was done. She entered the elevator and pressed "7" to head up to the conference room. She flashed a warm smile when she saw Dr. Harris, Dr. Jackson, and Shonda Roberts, an RN, seated at the dark, oval conference table.

She sat next to Shonda in the brown executive chair and placed her reports and black pen in front of her. Years ago, Shonda and Andrea had worked together at North Carolina Home Health.

When Shonda's car wasn't running, Andrea would pick her up for work and drop her kids off at school. Andrea left NCHH when she got the job at WMC, but she never forgot about Shonda though.

When a nursing position came open at WMC, she called Shonda and encouraged her to apply and use her as a reference. Shonda needed a better paying job so she could afford to take care of her four children.

Andrea put in a good word with the hiring manager and Shonda got the job! She had been there for almost a year and was now a part of Andrea's nursing team.

As Secretary Spates finished reading the minutes from the last meeting, Dr. Gray shuffled his way to the front of the room. He was careful not to bang his stubby legs into the chairs. He tugged on the knotted navy tie that seemed to be choking the air from his windpipe.

He had put on a lot of weight since his divorce. He was breathless by the end of the short walk to small podium. When he

42

caught his breath he said, "Good morning Dream Team of WMC!", Andrea slowly clapped her hands out of sync with the rest of the committee.

"My wonderful assistant is distributing this morning's agenda. We are going to focus on integrating the patient satisfaction questionnaire with the check-out process." The data shows that we're improving, but I would like to see an increase," said Dr. Gray.

Dr. Mark Gray was the clinical director and was Andrea's direct supervisor. She wouldn't say that they had the best relationship, nor would she say they had the worst. However, she didn't like being around him longer than she had to.

She couldn't stand how he treated nurses! - like they were second-class employees. Some would say he didn't value anything about you unless the letters, "MD" were behind your name. When Andrea made a suggestion, of any kind, his reply was,

"Well, you know we have to keep our MDs happy. If they don't like it here, you won't like it here."

She wished Dr. Gray would find a new place of employment, far, far away from Charlotte, but she just rolled with it. She knew she was an amazing nurse and team leader and no one, not even the precious MDs, could tell her otherwise.

Surprisingly, the meeting flowed smoothly without much discord. At twelve-forty-five, Dr. Gray banged his gavel and the meeting was adjourned. With her mind fixed on lunch, Andrea turned in her reports, briefly chatted with her colleagues, then started towards the exit.

Just as she was about to escape, an annoying voice said, "Andrea, meet me in my office in ten."

'Just great. I wonder what he needs to discuss that he didn't in the last forty-five minutes! - Ugh!', she thought.

Andrea rushed to her office, locked her things in the desk drawer, grabbed a protein bar and headed for Dr. Gray's office. When she arrived, he was sitting in his office chair with an arrogant smirk on his face.

He motioned his chubby hand towards one of the brown leather chairs in front of his desk and said,

"Have a seat. I have a quick phone call to make. Give me one moment," as he placed the phone receiver to his ear.

Masking her annoyance with a cool, calm, collected smile and a nod of approval she thought, 'Really... I'm missing my lunch for this nonsense?!

Dr. Bryant pressed the button labeled, "Speaker" and placed the receiver on the base.

"Uhh, Andrea, I have Mya from Human Resources on the phone joining in on this conversation - Is that ok with you?"

Suddenly, Andrea's mind was flooded with, 'Why does this fool have Mya from HR on the phone? I hope to God that this isn't what I think it is!'

Andrea simply responded, "Yes."

"Well, I've been looking over the customer satisfaction surveys from the past year and the numbers are not up to par in the nursing department."

WOMAN TAKE OFF YOUR CAPE

"Since I've been in this position, I have implemented evidence-based practices and patients are more satisfied with their wait times – the numbers *are* improving."

"Well, they aren't improving as fast as they should. Therefore, I had to make changes starting from the top - today is your last day at WMC."

"I've only been in this position for six months! The director *before* me had this position for THREE YEARS! How can firing me fix a problem that started *before* me?!"

"Well, it just boils down to business and numbers. You aren't the best fit for the direction the company is moving in," Dr. Gray said with a sarcastic undertone.

Andrea rose to her feet and questioned,

"So, my flawless attendance record, countless overtime hours, and commitment to providing OUTSTANDING care doesn't count for anything? You just said in the meeting that things are improving - this isn't a business move, THIS IS PERSONAL!

"Andrea, you need to calm down and just accept...,"

"Just accept?... Just accept what? Accept that you had a problem with me from Day One?! You may not like me, but I go above and beyond to perform my job on the highest level!" My evaluations prove that!

"Well, your termination is effective immedi..."

Andrea stormed out of the office door. A security officer was standing there to escort her to her office. Infuriation and embarrassment coursed through her veins.

She hurriedly collected her things from the desk drawer and turned over her keys and badge.

'How could they do this to me?' she thought as she fought back tears. Shonda stood staring from the nurses' station as Andrea walked the hallway holding a cardboard box filled with pieces of her career at WMC. She didn't utter a word.

With a security guard standing near, Andrea's hands trembled as she signed the termination documents. The HR manager handed her a pink carbon copy. She shoved the paper into the box and followed the guard to the parking garage.

The car door seemed to weigh a ton when she opened it. She flung the cardboard box onto the passenger seat and tossed the pink slip into the glove compartment. Her sky-blue scrubs seemed to sink her deep into the driver's seat. Her eyes welled with tears and her lips trembled like she was freezing cold.

Thoughts about everything and nothing bounced around the lobes of her brain. She couldn't bring herself to call Mike – she was speechless. In the still silence, she sat there sobbing through a whirlwind of heartache and fury.

At two-thirty-seven, she took a few deep breaths, brushed her palms across her face, and began the drive home. Her mind was so absent, she nearly passed the driveway.

No one else was at home this time of day. Mike was meeting with some clients and the kids were at school. She carried her broken heart into the upstairs shower.

She turned the knob and pulled the lever; her tears fell as fast as the water from the shower head. She pushed her back against the gray subway tiles and wailed, "How could he do that to me?! How could he do *us* like that?!"

They had just become homeowners last year. When Andrea got the new position at WMC, Mike quit his job in customer service and started his real estate business. After years of working hard and sacrificing, they were finally only a stable path... or so she thought.

She stepped out of the shower, dried off, and threw on her terry cloth robe. She reached to the bottom of her purse for her cell phone. She could feel a lump in her throat as she dialed Mike's number and fought back tears.

"Hey babe," Mike answered in his naturally charming voice.

With tears in her eyes Andrea responded, "They fired me!"

"What?! You gotta be kidding me, babe? How?... Why?", Mike asked.

"Can... Can you please just come home?", Andrea requested.

Mike replied, "Sure, I'll be there as soon as I'm done with this client. I love you Babe. Everything is going to be fine."

"I love you, too. See you soon," said Andrea.

She needed to tell her girls the news. She didn't think she could hold up over the phone, so she sent a message to the group chat,

"Hey ladies, he finally won... Dr. Gray fired me today."

The chat began flooding with messages like,

THE STRONG DON'T SURVIVE

"Oh, "H" to the no!"

"Are you serious?!"

"You were the best nurse that place ever seen!"

"Let us know if you need anything!"

Andrea messaged, "Brandy, is there anything I can do legally?"

Brandy responded, "Friend, it would be a hard case to fight since you signed that contract. Either party could terminate the position at any time... I'll see what I can do."

The ladies texted their goodbyes and Andrea buried herself under her favorite throw, as tears erupted sporadically. Soon, she drifted off to sleep.

Mike carefully opened the front door and tiptoed towards the couch. Andrea was still sleeping there from the night before. He sat quietly next to her, making certain to not wake her. He had gotten the kids dressed, dropped them off to school and came back to check on Andrea.

Their nine-year marriage had a turbulent past. They constantly argued and resented each other for not being where they wanted to in life.

Around the time of their second anniversary, they were both racing to the courthouse for a divorce. Just two weeks after Andrea started her search for a divorce lawyer, she discovered she was pregnant with Bryson.

That literally changed them both. They realized that it wasn't just about them anymore. They promised each other to put in the work to make their marriage happy and healthy.

48

Sometimes, Andrea felt Mike didn't support her ambitions, but she loved him and was committed to make it work.

As the sunlight touched her caramel tinted face, Mike stared at her and contemplated the right words to say to comfort her. When her dad passed away, he bought her sunflowers and her favorite sushi rolls. He knew how to take care of her *physically* but, words just weren't his thing.

Andrea opened her eyes to Mike's voice saying, "Good morning Babe, how are you feeling?"

"I…I feel like I'm in a bad dream. I just can't believe I got fired - just doesn't make sense…"

"We'll figure it out - I promise. You'll find something even better. I know you will," Mike reassured her.

"My years of hard work went down the drain in a matter of five minutes… just unbelievable," said Andrea while staring at the red accent wall.

When the quietness of the house hit her ears, she asked, "What time is it? Where are the kids?"

"It's almost nine. I took 'em to school already. Trust me, we're gonna to be fine. You need anything before I leave?"

'Before you leave? My heart was ripped from my chest just yesterday! I need you here with me! Can't you rearrange your schedule? Isn't that supposed to be a *perk* of real estate?', was what she wanted to say, but instead she mumbled,

"Okay."

"You know what I always say, "If my clients ain't happy, my pockets ain't happy." I'll check in with you around

49

lunch," replied Mike."

Andrea folded her arms and stared deeper into the red accent wall. Mike gathered his briefcase, kissed her on the forehead, and hurried towards the door. As the *click clack* of Mike's hard bottoms faded from the room, she felt abandoned.

Strong Hold

The bedroom was pitch black and quiet. She couldn't remember the last time she ate or if she showered the day before. There was an occasional beam of light whenever her cell phone buzzed on the nightstand.

"*Bzzt, bzzt.*" She glanced over at the screen as she lied in bed, hoping someone would call to offer her a job. She read the notification on her screen - it was from Regional Hospital!

She thought, '*This could be it*'! She pressed the envelope shaped icon and tightly clinched her eyes shut. She slowly lifted her eyelids and read, "Thank you for your interest. We regret to inform you... yada, yada, yada!"

Over the past six months, she had submitted at least a hundred applications. Although the emails were worded differently, they all read the same - she couldn't even get an interview!

She reached out to Shonda a few days after her termination thinking that Shonda would give her the "tea" on what was really going on at WMC. Shonda never bothered to respond to her. She never imagined that Shonda would turn her back on her.

She hadn't really heard from Kristin or Brandy much either. She picked up KJ from afterschool on Tuesdays and dropped him off at home, but she and Kristin didn't have any deep conversations.

Brandy called a few weeks ago to get some advice about whether she should take "Gym Dude" as her date to the North Carolina Law Society Scholarship Ball and to see how many tickets Andrea had sold for the event.

Andrea tried throwing hints about her feelings to her friends by saying things like, "I can't remember the last time I felt like getting dressed up" or "I guess I'm not meant to be a nurse."

Her words flew right over their heads because they would respond with, "It'll get better" or "You'll be fine". She felt like Bruce Willis on the *Sixth Sense*, like she was present, but no one truly saw her. They couldn't see her crying herself to sleep, struggling to get out of bed every day, or that she barely ate…not even Mike.

Mike was laser focused on growing his business. He talked to her about the kids, his work, and how much they had left in savings. Once she mentioned to him that she was feeling sad, he responded, "It'll get better Babe!"

Andrea fidgeted with the rose-colored phone case. Reluctantly, she scrolled through her contacts and pressed, "MAMA" - what did she have to lose?

"Hello… is that you Drea?", answered Beverly.

"Yes Mama. It's me," Andrea replied. Whew! I'm glad it's you and not one of those telemarket- scam-people! I can't tell who's calling me with this new phone!"

"Mama, just save my number so you'll know it's me. I called because I want to talk to you about something…

something important," Andrea replied.

"Ok..."

"I...I...I think I may be depressed," said Andrea.

"Depressed?... Really?... You just need to get out the house or find a hobby or..."

"Mama, it's not that simple. Most days I don't want to get out of bed. I tried to go to the grocery store the other day and guess what happened?"

"What?"

"I was minding my business, trying to just get a few things for the kids' lunches and get out. Well, here comes one of my old patients, Kathy, zigzagging her cart down the bread aisle."

"I tried to cover my face inside my jacket - it didn't work."

She shouted and waved, "Hey Nurse A!" and walked up to me.

"I said, "Hi Ms. Kathy, I'm actually running late..."

"I can't believe they fired you like that- you were one of the best ones!", she said.

She didn't stop there, "You don't look like yourself – you found another job yet?"

I felt like I wanted to vomit right there in the aisle!

I told her, "I'm just taking my time looking."

"Then, she had the nerve to shove two bottles in my face and ask, 'Which one of these is good for a headache, a temperature, and a cough?'! "

"If it weren't for the kids - sometimes I don't see the point of living anymore..."

"Andrea, I know you're stronger than that! You just gonna let some rude old lady make you depressed?", asked Beverly.

"Mama, it's not just that... I dedicated my whole life to nursing and now this? - No one will hire me!"

"I don't know how we're going to make ends meet... Mike can't do it by himself - I'm so tired, Mama," Andrea explained.

"Well, Mike just needs to get a second job!", replied Beverly.

"Mama, I just need you to show me, *your daughter*, some support! You *never* come visit me – just to spend time with me," said Andrea.

"I can't do it this month. You know the Women's Society anniversary is coming up – it's a celebration all this month! - remember, you helped me decorate last year?

"Yes Mama, I remember," Andrea answered.

"Oh that reminds me, you think I should wear my black, lacy dress or the emerald green one? You know, the one with the side split? Maybe I should get something new - Andrea, you still there?

"You should probably wear the black one. You can't go wrong with black for an evening event," Andrea replied, trying to swallow the lump swelling in her throat.

"Yeah, that would look really good with my hair up and my silver heels - whatchu' think?"

"That would look great Mama… I-I think I'm going to lay down, I have a mild headache," Andrea said, with blurred eyes.

"Ok. I'll send you pictures of the dresses so you can help me make a final decision - talk to you later," replied Beverly.

"Bye Mama," the tears fell onto the bed sheets as Andrea pressed the red icon to end the call.

"MAMA, WHY DON'T YOU UNDERSTAND?!", she screamed as she buried her face hard into the satin pillowcase.

Andrea laid there on the tear-soaked pillow, trying to recall a time her mother had been there for her emotionally. Well, when Bentley James dumped her junior year, she sent tulips with a card that read, "You're strong, this won't break you."

She remembered standing at the gravesite after her father's funeral. Beverly placed her hand on Andrea's shoulder and whispered, "Don't let them see you crying, you have to be strong for the rest of them."

Andrea's heart longed to be understood – by anyone. No one truly understood, but they all thought they did. Everyone went on with their lives, oblivious to the pain she felt.

"I know I'm supposed to be strong, but just can't!", she cried. "God, I can't pull myself out! I need help!", she said as she rocked back and forth, holding herself in a fetal position.

She felt that God couldn't hear her prayers anymore. She threw the gray covers over her tear stained face and tossed herself from one side to the other.

She reached inside the top drawer of the nightstand and grabbed a pen and a rose-colored notebook. It had been months since she poured her feelings onto those pages, but it always made her feel better.

She walked across the cold kitchen tiles and down the steps into the two-car garage. The tension began to evaporate from her shoulders and back as she reclined the leather driver's seat. With each stroke of the ballpoint pen, she felt more at peace.

Too Strong

'Dang, it's crowded in here,' Mike said to himself as he waited in line at *The Fresh Express*. It was worth the wait though. He was going to surprise Andrea with a steaming bowl of lobster bisque, a garden salad, and a spinach and turkey wrap.

Between gym, work, and the kids, he hadn't spent much time with her. He knew she was feeling a little down on herself, but her favorite lunch would help that.

"Number two eighty!"

Mike checked his receipt and raised his hand as he walked to the register on the right. He showed the blond-haired women his receipt and she handed him the white paper bag from the counter.

"Thanks!", he said as he rushed towards the exit.

Mike pulled into the driveway beaming from ear-to-ear over surprising Andrea with a lunch date. He walked over to the passenger side of the luxury car to get the food, but the humming engine from the garage distracted him.

Through the garage window, he could see the taillights from Andrea's car glaring red. 'She must be headed to the store,' he thought. He didn't want the surprise ruined so he ran to the garage door and punched in the code, "0209", their wedding anniversary.

The garage door lifted and Mike scurried to the passenger side window and hollered,

"Surprise Babe!" Andrea was speechless!

She didn't say a word, she just sat there… with her eyes closed and her head hung, chin to chest. Mike placed his hand on her chest -it didn't rise or fall. She was as cold as a dark winter's night.

"Oh my God oh my God oh my God!", Mike shouted.

His heart pounded and his legs moved as fast as a cheetah towards the driver's side door. He shut off the engine and eased Andrea onto the garage floor.

His hands trembled as he placed them on the front of her neck - he couldn't find a pulse. He yanked his phone from his back pocket and dialed 9-1-1. He placed the phone on the floor and his strong hands on Andrea's chest as the operator walked him through the steps of CPR.

Flashing lights and wailing sirens could be heard at every house on Hilltop Lane. Time stood still as Mike watched the EMT hook his wife up to the machines. The ambulance doors

56

closed in slow motion as Mike watched his wife lay there, cold and lifeless.

Mike paced the corridors of the cold hospital waiting for an update on Andrea's condition. A doctor with broad shoulders and dark hair approached Mike as he stood near the vending machines biting his nails.

"Mr. Jones, we did all we could to revive your wife. Her body just couldn't recover from the damage."

"Nah, Nah…wait a minute - you're telling me my wife is gone?"

"Mr. Jones, I'm very sorry."

"NO! NO! HOW DID THIS HAPPEN?!", Mike shouted tearfully.

The doctor replied, "Mr. Jones, your wife died due to carbon monoxide poisoning."

"HOW?! WHY?!", Mike said, shaking his head uncontrollably.

The doctor escorted Mike to a nearby lobby area and offered him a bottle of water. A bearded man approached him,

"Mr. Jones, I'm sorry about your wife. I'm Investigator McCall with FPD."

"I want to speak with you concerning some of the details involving your wife's death. Do you mind if we speak here?", the investigator.

"N-No, I-I don't mind," said Mike as he blotted his eyes with the back of his wrist.

"We have reason to believe your wife's death was a suicide. This is a copy of the note we found underneath the driver's seat."

Mike's knees buckled underneath him as soon as his fingertips touched the folded pink paper.

"Oh My God oh my God - WHY WOULD YOU THIS ANDREA?!", Mike screamed.

A trail of tears streaked his face like rain on a windshield as he read his wife's final words:

To The Loves of My Life,

I love you with everything in me. You deserve so much better than what I can give you. This pain has made me a terrible mom and wife to you all. You deserve so much more than I have to give. I don't deserve to have you as my family. I know each of you will have a happier life without me in it. This pain just won't leave me, I've tried and it just won't. I want the best for ALL of you. I can never be what's best for you. Please don't worry about me. I want you all to laugh together and have a good life. Bryson, I'm so proud of you. Always protect your little sister. She looks up to you. Olivia, keep being the beautiful, kind, intelligent girl that you are. Both of you, love, honor and respect your dad. He loves you very much. Mike, I love you. Move forward with your life and keep loving the kids. I didn't do this because of any of you. I did this because of me. I just can't go on living like this. I love you always, and forever Mike, Olivia, and Bryson...sorry for leaving like this.

-Andrea

6 The Strong Woman

Faster than Usain Bolt, the Strong Woman is always there to answer the call! She'll walk through the frigid cold, the flames of Hell, and high water to save the day!

Need someone to wipe your tears after your goldfish died? Call the Strong Woman. Need someone to carry your boxes from the moving truck? Call the Strong Woman. Need someone to file your taxes? You got it, CALL THE STRONG WOMAN! She's built to handle *any* situation so, she'll *never* need your help... She's got it all under control!

With the Cape of Dependability on her shoulders and a mask to shield her face, she plays the role of "leaning post" and she is the "wind beneath the wings" of those who call her *Mom, Wife, Companion, Daughter, Friend, Colleague, and Stranger.* But that's just it...she's playing a role.

Don't get me wrong, the Strong Woman has a heart of gold, but she's following the script that has been given to her by the people in her life. Without hesitation, her circle unanimously chooses her for this character because they know she will deliver…Every. Single. Time.

The Strong Woman is committed to her work, dedicated to her family, and loyal to her friends. She's often thought of as "The Strong One" or the "Mama" of the group. The word "*no*" is obsolete in her vocabulary. She'll give away her hard-earned money or the shirt from her back without batting an eye.

Just like Andrea, she goes above and beyond to make sure that she is there for EVERYONE, except herself. Being the strong woman that she is, she has a way of making her juggling act appear effortless. She shows up dressed in a heroic smile, a positive attitude, and a glorious Cape of Strength flowing behind her.

The reality is, her cape is so dang heavy she can barely walk, let alone fly! Somehow, she pushes pass the weight of the load and her own needs to provide what others expect from her. The certainty of knowing that her good deeds will come back to her when she needs it most, helps keep the Strong Woman going. The harsh reality is, the story almost *never* goes that way for the Strong Woman.

When she needs someone to be strong for her, will it be well received? Most of the time, The Strong Woman's needs won't even be acknowledged! Needing help is not a super-power of *The All-Saving Strong Woman*! The people she rescues are not accustomed to *her* needing anything so most likely, they won't offer her anything - that's not a part of the script! The Strong Woman plays the role of swooping in to save *them*, NOT the other way around.

Sooner or later, the Strong Woman discovers that the only person to rescue her when her world has turned upside is not the person she has been rescuing. The Strong Woman's savior *is* the Strong Woman. Unfortunately, this reality does not become apparent until after the damage has been done to the Strong Woman's health. In worse cases, like Andrea's, the damage consumes the Strong Woman's will to live.

The Healthy Truth About Andrea

When Andrea was terminated from her dream job, her circle assumed that she would carry herself from the burning building of painful emotions she was trapped inside of. So many times, they had seen her do it - for them and her patients. At most, they thought sprinkling a few words of encouragement would be enough to help her douse the flames.

Andrea's circle displayed a lack of urgency to the devastation and hopelessness she experienced after suffering a big loss. This lack of response is not uncommon among the friends and family of the Strong Woman.

Andrea felt like she was literally drowning as the waves of life began to overtake her. As the waves crashed and beat against her, she cried out,"Help Me! Save Me!". She cried out through her silence and subtle hints, but no one was there to throw her a life raft. In fact, family and friends didn't even notice she was in danger.

Unfortunately, overwhelming emotions can lead to clinical depression and in cases like Andrea's, suicide. In the past year, 17.7 million adults experienced at least one major depressive episode (4). As defined by the National Institute of Mental Health, depression is a common mood disorder.

Depression causes severe symptoms that impact the way you think, feel, and go about your day-to-day life (5). It can be difficult to identify that you may be depressed, especially if you're the Strong Woman.

Each person that battles depression has a different experience. That is why there are a variety of symptoms that can be experienced by an individual's suffering from depression. In order to be diagnosed with depression, some (not all) of the following symptoms must be present:

A sad or empty feeling that won't go away

 Feeling hopeless, helpless, worthless, guilty or having negative thoughts that persist

 Loss of interest in things that you used to enjoy (hobbies, sex, etc.)

 Feeling restless yet fatigue

 Difficulty with concentrating, remembering things, or decision making

 Changes in appetite or weight changes

 No rhyme or reason for aches and pains, cramps, or digestive problems that don't get better with treatment

 Thoughts of death, suicide or a suicide attempt

 Thoughts of death, suicide or a suicide attempt

It's important to remember that not ALL symptoms have to be present to experience depression. As you read the list, you probably said, "Everyone has probably felt like this at some point in their lives." You are right, they probably have. However, the difference with depression is those feelings are persistent and last for weeks to years.

With depression, you can't *think* yourself happy. You can't just say to yourself, "Sis, shake it off!" and it goes away. Depression is a serious medical condition that should be treated with the same urgency as getting hit in the head with a bat.

It would be hard for you or anyone to ignore the blood cascading down your forehead, the throbbing headache, or the stitches you would need to close the wound. In most cases, symptoms of depression don't come with physical signs that can be seen by anyone.

I believe it's safe to say that everyone who is living in this world can be at risk for depression at any given moment. However, women are twice as likely to suffer from depression. Suffering a major loss (death of a loved one, job, home), a major life change, physical trauma or illness, stress, or certain medications can trigger an episode of depression (5). If you have family members who have experienced depression or other mental illnesses, you are more at risk.

If you experience depression, you may feel the need to look to family for consolation or understanding. There is nothing wrong with wanting to lean on someone you love. However, don't make the mistake of expecting your friends and family to respond appropriately or say something that cures your depression. Your

Aunt Jackie or your girl Jennifer are not mental health professionals!

Your doctor and/or a licensed mental health professional went through years of training to treat your depression, not Aunt Jackie. Besides, if you're usually Jennifer's go-to-girl for an emotional crisis, it's highly unlikely she will acknowledge the severity of your mental state or have the right words to say.

Of all mental illnesses, depression is the most common and it should be taken seriously. If you have any of these risk factors along with symptoms that won't go away, please make an appointment with your doctor. Most likely, your doctor will have you complete a questionnaire and take a full history of what you have been experiencing and feeling.

Your doctor will then recommend treatment options in the form of anti-depressant medication, counseling, or a combination of the two. Once you have been diagnosed with depression, it's important to follow the recommendations of your doctors. Just like with anything else, it takes time for therapies to be effective. It can take up to 4 weeks for anti-depressants to alter the chemicals in your brain.

Counseling or behavioral therapy may take several sessions before you notice a difference in how you feel. Be consistent about your health! Whether it's making sure you take your anti-depressant daily, daily journaling, or self-care, make your well-being a top priority!

Each year, there are close to 800,000 suicides world-wide. For every person that dies by suicide, there are 20 people who have attempted suicide (6). Depression is a risk factor for suicide. If you or anyone you know is experiencing any of the following symptoms, IMMEDIATELY call the National Suicide Prevention Lifeline (1-800-273-TALK (8255) or text the Crisis Text Line (741741):

 Feelings of having no reason to live or frequent talks about dying

 Making plans to kill themselves like buying a gun or researching ways to kill themselves (online and/or books)

 Feeling like there's no solution or like they are stuck

 Withdrawing from family or friends

 More frequent drug or alcohol use

 Feeling guilty, ashamed, or like a burden

 Going from 0 to 100 feeling very happy, very sad, or very angry

 Taking dangerous risks

 A change in sleeping or eating habits

 Giving away prized possessions

 Saying final goodbyes or making a will (in combination with other symptoms)

If you are experiencing symptoms of suicide, please don't take it lightly. This is like having a head-on collision with life - it's an emergency! This is not the time to brush the dust from your cape and keep flying. If you are having thoughts of ending your life or you have made an attempt to end your life, you must get help immediately!

If you're at this point, I'm hoping that your family and friends will help you through this. However, they may not. They may think, "She's just venting" or "She's just a little down". Well, it really doesn't matter if they understand what you are going through or not. You must save yourself! Remove the cape and go get help! You are more than worth it!

7 The Superpower of "No"

The Earth stops spinning on its axis, lightning bolts crack the sky and crash against the ground causing the entire world to go up in flames. That's what you believe will happen if you tell them "No" - Right?

For some reason, Strong Women think that a *no* from them pushes the start button for Armageddon. Why do you feel the need to grant everyone's wishes? I know you tell yourself things like, "I'm just doing what I would want someone to do for me" or you say, "They really need me." I believe in the Golden Rule, too, but it does not mean that those two letters can never part your lips.

Stop convincing yourself into thinking that always saying "yes" is the right thing to do. Saying yes to every request that comes your way is the gateway to depression! You can recover from the stress associated with saying "yes" in moderation.

However, if *yes* spills from your mouth like water from a busted fire hydrant, it will drain the life from you! When it gets to this point, the simple things in your life can become overwhelming and important relationships can become strained.

Don't fear telling them *no* – and meaning it! Saying no is one of your most valuable superpowers. It allows you to set boundaries that protect you from the physical and mental wear and tear that comes with saying *yes* all the time.

I'm not saying that you should *never* save the day for others. But what I *am* saying is, saving someone else's day should not be more important than saving your own. If you're always busy pouring into everyone, even strangers you meet in the grocery store, you will pour yourself empty. When you're all poured out like a little teapot, it's likely that you won't be able to find someone to pour into you.

That is why you must learn to pour into yourself Strong Woman! Buuuuut, it's impossible to do that without saying "no". How do you say "no"? Oh, let me count the ways!

Imagine this: The person you have the toughest time saying "no" to just asked you for whatever it is they always ask you for. Now, pretend as if you are responding back to them. Read each one of this aloud:

"I know I usually do it, but I'm not going to be able to do it this time."

"I'm in bed at the time of night."

"I'm under doctor's care, so, I can't come."

"I don't have the extra money to buy that right now."

"You know, if you look it up online, there's instructions on how to do it."

"No."

It's that simple! Even if it wasn't simple for you today, practice makes perfect! I'm not saying that you should shut down every request that comes your way, but you wouldn't be reading this book if you were using the "Superpower of No" enough.

Declining to grant someone's wishes isn't the only way to use the "Superpower of No". In order to save yourself, you must say "no" to negativity as well. Negativity can come in the form of thoughts about yourself that tear down and instead of uplift. These thoughts can come from within or be planted by a person, music, movies, social media, or an event from your past or present.

Clearing your mind and spirit of things that do not promote positivity in your life will lower your risk of suffering from depression. In order to do this, it's important for you to find ways to express how you feel and what you think. The reality is, the people who you love and trust the most, like family and friends, may not be the best people to vent to.

Although they may mean well, sometimes their words can add to the load you're already carrying. Find a licensed therapist, counselor, or spiritual leader that can help you sort out your emotions. This way, you won't have to worry about your private feelings being discussed at the next family gathering.

You're so used to being strong for others, you may find it difficult to open up and talk about how you feel. Not only that, it may be difficult for you identify your true feelings because you have grown accustomed to overlooking them. Even if you don't mind opening up, you may have a hard time trusting someone with your innermost thoughts and feelings.

This is why journaling is such a powerful tool for the Strong Woman. Journaling will allow you to get your thoughts and feelings outside of your head and heart, and into a safe place where you can be open and honest.

After I journal, I find that I'm more relaxed and that I can push the reset button on my thoughts and feelings. Journaling can help you "unpack" and organize your feelings before you express them in a conversation. Scheduling time to journal on a daily or weekly basis is a great way to pour time and energy into YOU!

Strong Woman, the secret lies in learning to say no and reserving some of your time, energy, and money for yourself. That way, you are never empty! Embrace the reality that you may not be able to save everyone - and that's ok. Just make sure that you save yourself.

8 Hustle and Bust-le

❝ You see…that sign right there in the back?! The s*ign* says these shoes are buy one get one free! - and now you wanna charge me full price? This is a scaaandalou*s* shame!"

The old lady's top lip curled as she sucked her teeth and gave me the "if-looks-could-kill" stare through her oversized bifocals. Ughh, just five more minutes in this living Hell they call *Shoe Paradise!*

I buried my, "you-gettin'-on-my-last-nerves tone" before I responded back.   Instead, I used my, "the- customer-is-always-right" voice,

"Ma'am, the black loafers are *not* a part of the sale - it's printed at the bottom of the sign."

Something told me she wasn't going to accept the fact that the shoes were *not* on sale.   Well, what something told me was right.

With her fists pressed up against her hips and her head swiveling all over the place she yelled,

"These shoes cost an arm and a leg! - all of 'em should be on sale! This is a scandal *and* a shame!"

No, you gray-haired bobble head, *you* are the scandal *and* the shame! - is what I wanted to say, but I couldn't, so I tried to reason with her,

"Ma'am, you can purchase the red pair, get the brown ones for free, and buy the black ones when they go on sale in the off sea -"

"Well, I don't think that's right! You have this BIG RED SIGN, sitting in front of *all* the shoes! They should *all* be on sale! - Let me speak to your manager!"

Could somebody *PLEASE* come and get this old battle ax out of this store?! - Ughhh! This old devil is about to have me late picking my kids up from after school. I can't afford to pay late fees on the account of her being illiterate - the sign is clear as day!

"No problem ma'am - I'll page him right now."

I could see Marcus walking to the front of the store. He must've overheard the situation because his eyes were stretched as wide as this lady's foot and his neck was as stiff as her wig.

He signaled for me to go clock out while he took care of the *She Devil* who was standing at the register with her arms folded - Thank you, God!

I power walked to the clock, punched in my code and ran to my car. Seventeen minutes wasn't enough time for me to get to after school without getting charged a late fee.

Well, at least it wouldn't be due until the next cycle. Working full-time, raising two energetic boys, and taking 3 classes at TCC was taking a toll on me. It was all going to pay off soon though…

The day I walk into *Shoe Paradise,* throw my hands in the air and shout from the depths of my soul, "I QUIT!" will be a dream come true! I hope *She Devil* is there to see it so she'll know she can't terrorize me anymore. Then, I could get a good paying job - one without annoying customers who are never satisfied.

"Hi Ms. Erica! Kenneth and Kevin are on their way from the art room," the after-school director said as I rushed through the door.

I glanced at my phone … 5:58 pm.

Take that after school! No late fees today!

In an all-out sprint, I could see my boys running towards the cafeteria. Kenny had probably challenged Kev to a race for who was going to ride in the front seat. I could tell by the pout on Kev's face that Kenny would be riding shotgun.

Kev rushed to the check-out table with a green piece of construction paper in hand,

"Mama, look at what I made!"

"Oooh, that's nice!"-I didn't have a clue what it was.

"Kenny made a cool dinosaur, too!"

"Hey, Ma," Kenny said in a dry, "I'm-too-big-for-this-art-project-crap" voice.

He hated afterschool since he was a *big* 5th grader now. I told him I needed him to stay to keep an eye on his little brother.

The truth was, I didn't have any other options My cousin Brea lived close to the school, but I wouldn't let her take care of an imaginary pet!

Bustled in Love

"My team is *bigger* and *stronger*! They are going to beat your sorry team!"

"Nu -uh because the Gators are faster and your team is stupid!", yelled Kev as he folded his little arms.

"Ok, ok boys, you can talk football, but you can't yell and say words like *stupid*...Got it?"

"Yes ma'am", they said in harmony.

We drove back to our two-bedroom apartment, with football trash talk flying across the car seats. My boys loved playing football with the Little League on Saturdays. It sucked that their dad never bothered to show up to any of their games.

I hated myself for having kids with a man like that. In my defense, he was full of promise when we first met... I remember everything about that day.

I was standing in the hallway talking to my girl Denise and this tall, athletic, seventeen -year old, with the smoothest brown skin you ever seen, asked me to go the homecoming dance with him.

I should've known he wouldn't be any good right then and there! - What seventeen -year old has *perfect* skin? Anyway, for me, it was love at first sight. A fine, senior on the basketball team asking me, a sophomore, to the dance - you couldn't tell me that I wasn't *that girl*!

Shoot, I felt like Sanaa Lathan in *Love and Basketball*, 'cept I was a cheerleader. He most definitely had that Omar Epps vibe about him – cool, smooth, and oh so fine!

The lil' heiffas at school couldn't stand me! They rolled their eyes and sucked their teeth when they saw me strolling through the halls with Kennon Thompson -I didn't care!

A part of me liked that they were jealous. They looked sick with envy when they saw me strutting through the halls with Kennon's strong arm thrown across my shoulder like a mink shawl - We were celebrities!

Back then, I would daydream about our life for hours! I would close my eyes and see us sitting on the back patio of our nice brick house, drinking sweet tea as we watched our children play on the two point five acres of fresh cut green grass - I was so in love with him!

When Kennon left Brooksville High, The Ville as we called it, I never went out with, kissed, or even *looked* at another dude. Now him on the other hand - that's a whole-nother story.

Kennon went to LCC, a community college in Louisiana, on a basketball scholarship. I remember begging my sister, Crystal, to buy me a Greyhound ticket so I could go visit him. It was on one of those visits to his apartment that I got pregnant with Kenny.

Mama never approved of Kennon so, me getting knocked up cut her that much deeper. It hurt us both when he denied that Kenny was his baby. He wasn't even there the day he was born, but his mom was.

She examined Baby Kenny's face for what seemed like hours. I watched her uncurl his tiny little fingers and with one look she said, "This is my grandson!"

After two years of barely passing classes and a torn ACL, Kennon lost his scholarship and moved back to Tennessee. With Mama by my side and a chunky little 3-month-old in my arms, I graduated from The Ville that same year.

Boy, I didn't waste no time moving out to go "shack up" with Kennon, as Mama called it. She was totally against it and told me to stay at home with her, go to TCC, and take care of the baby. Shoot, I was a grown woman - she couldn't tell me what to do!

Well, my "grown-woman- ness" backfired big time. Living with Kennon was nothing like what I daydreamed about in high school. I worked a bunch dead end jobs and Kennon spent most of the money he made from the car dealership on gambling. Back then, I didn't wanna admit it, but my life was going nowhere real fast.

I wasn't his *Brown Shuga* or his *Angel Face* like back at The Ville. Instead, he called me *"Ugly -Stupid- Hoe"* more times than I can count. I just took it though – took it because I wanted us to be a *real* family.

One day, after a heart-to-heart with Mama , I decided to leave Kennon for good. I had started packing our stuff into old shoe boxes, garbage bags, and a raggedy suitcase.

Out of nowhere, I got sick to my stomach and threw up on the bathroom floor. My plans to leave were canceled – I was pregnant with Kev.

Bang! Bam! Bang! I'll never forget that day – my head knocked against the beige wall, over and over while Kennon squeezed my neck with his gigantic hands.

I can still see Kennon's warm, deep brown eyes overflow with rage when I threatened to take Kenny and move back in with Mama after a big argument.

He had shoved me a few times before, but nothing like this. I *literally* thought I was going to die! I can still remember trying to catch my breath and watching my baby sit on the couch screaming because he was so scared - that was the last straw.

I couldn't bear the thought of my boys being motherless or Mama having to bury me. So, I stuffed our clothes into three, black garbage bags and I left Kennon – left him sitting on that big, ugly, pleather couch, facing the wall he bashed my head against.

After I moved in with Mama, he would come by and spend time with the boys – pretending like he wanted to be a good dad and trying to get me to be his "Ugly-Stupid-Hoe" again.

When he saw his game and empty promises weren't working and that he couldn't win me back, the calls and visits became non-existent.

Now, he thinks somebody is supposed to give him a "Daddy of the Year Award" because he calls the boys on their birthdays and buys a present or two for Christmas - it's sad and pathetic!

"When we get in the house, what's the first thing you need to do?", I asked as we pulled into the parking lot.

Kev answered,

"PUT OUR HOMEWORK ON THE TABLE!"

I did this *Before-We-Go-In -The-House Quiz* every day so the boys wouldn't get distracted. I glanced over at Kenny, I tried to hold my breath to keep from laughing…"

"HA! Kenny, you are something else!"

He was looking at the dirty floormat with his cheek resting on his fist. He barely mumbled the answers to my quiz - the boy was tired of my foolishness!

I checked the boys' homework, pulled off Taco Tuesday with two kinds of shells, scrubbed the kitchen while they took their baths, said bedtime prayers, and kissed them both good night.

I only had two hours to finish and submit my homework online. I hate math and these algebraic equations were working my nerves on overtime!

I clicked *"Submit"* right at "11:57 pm, praying that I had enough answers right for at least a C minus – I needed this class to graduate!

My eyelids felt like thirty- pound weights and my feet hurt like I was the punter for my boys' football team –

"Shoot! They have football practice tomorrow!" I was almost too tired to shower, but I jumped in, cleaned the *important* parts really good, and jumped out.

Bzzzt, Bzzzt. It was my homegirl Sheena calling. I finished drying off and put the phone on speaker.

"Hey Bestie!", I answered, trying to hide the sleepiness in my voice.

"You sound like you haven't been to sleep all this year! – girl, you ok?", she asked.

I swear you couldn't get nothing past the Private "Eye" Sheena Smith! - She noticed *EV-ER-RY-THING!*

"I'm good - just been running all day, but what's been going on with you?", I asked, trying to speed up the conversation.

"Soooo, I was calling to see if you had bought your ticket for the *Black Diamonds and Gold Party.* You know it's about to be sold out, right?", she asked.

"I'm probably not going, I have so much to catch up on and my mid-terms start the week after –"

"Excuses, Excuses, EX-SCUSES! Girl, you *have* to come this year!"

"I haven't been to that in years – not since me and Kennon broke up…"

"That's *exactly* why you need to come! Today in the breakroom, I overheard Stacy and Monica say that Kennon was gonna to be there with his new boo - Kim!" she said in a voice that was too high-pitched for this time of night.

"Well, that's good for him! While he's out with this one and that one, I'm the only one worried about *our* kids!"

"That's why you need to get out the house friend! Kennon was the first *and* last man you had - well, he wasn't that much of a man, but you get what I'm saying! It's time for something shiny and brand-new!"

"The only "*men*" I have time for right now are Kenny and Kev. I'm not ready for the dating game anyway," I said, knowing full well that I was thinking about dating.

"I hope you change your mind about this party sis. I know the perfect dress for you to wear – a dress that will make Kim look like a washed- up background singer struggling to hit the high notes!"

"Girrrl, you gone make me wake up the kids!", I screamed with laughter, "Sheen, you so crazy! - that's why you my girl!"

I glanced at the time on the silver alarm clock, "I'll text you tomorrow girl, I need to get in this bed…Good night friend."

"Good night girl…text me tomorrow now!"

I already knew - I wasn't going to that party. I didn't have the money for hair, nails, or a dress to make Kim look like a washed-up backup singer.

Besides, I was going to be braiding hair that weekend, making a few coins instead of spending them. Even if I bought a ticket, I would feel guilty - that's money that could go on something my boys may need – or want.

I finished putting cocoa butter on my brown, cactus-haired legs and climbed into bed. I laid there staring into the pitch- black room….thinking… thinking about how I had to do this all over again tomorrow, and the next day, and the day after that – it didn't feel fair, but I'm all they got.

Smooth Hustle

"*Chirp, chirp. Tweet, tweet, tweet.*" The sound of the exotic birds of the Amazon rainforest was *not* soothing at five in the morning. I couldn't find the freakin' thing to shut it off!

I looked on the nightstand – nope. I searched on the dresser -nope. Dang, this thing was driving me crazier than a bed bug! I peeled back the covers – thank you God!

I quickly swiped it off, threw my feet onto the floor, and shuffled towards my backpack. I flipped the lights and caught a glimpse of my reflection in the full-length mirror next to my dresser.

Good Lord! I looked like a real-life zombie - straight outta *The Walking Dead*! I pulled *The Psychology of Man* book and a yellow highlighter from my backpack and plopped myself onto the queen-sized mattress.

I dozed and read about Pavlov's cat, dog, or whatever it was and before I knew it, it was time to wake the boys up. Thankfully, Kenny helped Kev get dressed while I packed snacks and a lunch for Kev. My little spoiled brat wouldn't eat anything from the cafeteria except for the oatmeal cookies and chocolate milk.

"Boys, you ready?"

I could hear Kenny telling Kev that he couldn't take Mr. Bo-Bo, this lil' raggedy giraffe he had since he was a baby, to school with him. I was preparing myself for whining and waterworks, but instead I heard Kev say,

"Ok, he can stay here and make sure nobody messes with my other toys while I'm at school".

"RRRight... grab your backpack, Mama is waiting on us," Kenny said as he stood in the doorway of their room.

"Awww, my boys look so handsome this morning! Here's your lunch Kev and here are the snacks for after school Kenny."

For *once* in our lives, we were on schedule to get to school *and* work on time, which was kinda unusual for a Wednesday.

No pee-soaked pajamas or I'm-too-cool-for-school attitude from Kenny. My boys are growing into fine young men -with or without Kennon.

Work Hustle

The nerve of these people! How did this man think he was going to return his shoes - *without* the shoes! I still had an hour 'til lunch and I was getting' sick and tired already! At least I could get a free lunch today.

The Work to Wellness Fair was going to be in the food court today. They came every year so we could decide on what insurance we wanted for the next year.

Either way, all of it was too expensive for me and the boys were on federal insurance. But, I was looking forward to the free T-shirts and a large- sized smoothie from *Smoothilicious*!

Dang! Apparently, everybody that worked at this mall wanted free lunch today. It was at least 200 people lined up for free cookies, pizza, and keychains. Well, I'm going straight to the smoothie line and get out of here!

"Hi, I'm Carla" said this short lady standing at the table covered in pink pencils and flyers.

While keeping my eyes on the prize, *Smoothilicious* that is, I said a quick, "Hi."

"Please take one of our bags - there's tons of info *and* goodies inside!" she said while gently pushing the bag into my hand.

"Ok...Thanks!" I took the bag and made a B-line towards the smoothie station.

Finally! I had my extra-large, oh so delicious Mango Tango! Shoot, I had to wait in line for about twenty minutes *and* have small talk with people who had other free food stuck in their teeth. I was going to enjoy every last bit of this hard-earned free smoothie.

I walked back to *Shoe Hell* as I sipped and ran through my To-Do-List in my head - Pick up the boys, football practice, cook dinner (well maybe *Chicken Charlies*) and take my psych test by midnight.

I sat on the black, metal bench and inhaled the scent of fresh baked cookies from the *Sweet Factory*. I wasn't about to clock in early, *Shoe Hell* got enough free work out of me – not today!

I sipped and studied this window shopper strolling along. She must've worked at a bank -or somewhere upscale. Her soft, cream blouse was tucked neatly into her tan dress pants. The gold buckle on her designer belt complemented her expensive earrings and necklace. She smiled here and there... probably thinking about all of her success and money. She was really pretty - and her butt wasn't even big! That's going to be me one day...

I stopped people-watching for a minute and dug through the bag *Little Miss Pushy* forced me into getting. Oooh, looky here! - chewing gum, hand sanitizer, and a little first aid kit thingy to put in my purse for Kenny and Kev - there was a lot of good stuff in here! I put the goodies in my purse and kept the bright colored brochures in the bag.

Only three more hours and I'm a free woman! ... well, at least 'til eight tomorrow morning. I hated working here so much it made me want to start back smoking which I quit right before I got pregnant with Kev. At least it was better than working at that convenience store being held at gun point! – now that was a hot, ratchet mess!

Hustled Out

I unlocked the dented door and threw my keys onto the little coffee table.

"Go straight to your room and don't come out until I say so!", I said pointing to the dinosaur covered bunk beds.

I can't believe the boys almost got into a fight on field today-with each other!

"But Mama, you said that we could play the game tonight,"

Kev said, with a lip so pouted it looked like it was filled with helium.

I stared him square in his puppy-dog eyes,

"NOW!"

"Awww, man!", he said, storming off to the room with Kenny following close behind.

See, that's why Kennon needs to bring his at-least-I-buy-Christmas-presents-sorry-excuse-for-a-dad- behind to the games! - Ughhh!!!

I will *never* understand how a person can *know* they have kids with *their blood* running through their veins and not show up for them! - Just abso-unbelievably stupid!

After the day I had, a hot shower and the bed was calling my name! I gave the boys a good talking to about their behavior and tucked them in – well, Kev anyway.

He was so cute saying, "I'm sorry for making you really sad Mama."

"I'm proud of you for being a big boy and saying you're sorry," I told him.

"I'm sorry, too Mama," Kenny said,

"You work really hard to take care of us - I'll do better as a big brother."

"You boys have to stick together. You can't fight each other, we're a team," I said looking at them both – they looked so much like Kennon.

"We love you Mama," they both said as I hugged them goodnight.

They weren't perfect, but they really were good kids - with they bad lil' butts!

I swear this day had been longer than them Pentecostal church services Mama made us go to! I got undressed and while the shower was getting hot, I remembered seeing this thing for the shower inside the plastic bag from Little Miss Pushy.

I dug around in the bag until I felt something with a hook on the end - found it! I stepped over the wall of the tub and hung the pink hanger over the shower head.

I could feel each drop bounce off my skin. I closed my eyes real tight and tears fell down my face like rain on a summer's day. I hoped that the steam would melt away the worries and struggles of being a single mother.

I was so tired - tired in my mind, my body, and my heart. It wasn't fair that my boys didn't have a dad in their lives! It wasn't fair that they couldn't look on the sidelines and hear him yelling, "Good tackle!" or "You got this!".

I'M NOT GIVIN' UP ON THEM! I'm gone make sure my kids get *everything* they deserve – daddy or no daddy! My tears turned into a full-on ugly cry. No matter what, I was going to keep pressing and pushing for Kenny and Kev to have a good life.

When I lifted my eyes, the pink hanger was staring back at me. I held my fingers close together and placed my fingertips at the top of my right breast.

I started moving my fingers in a circular motion… I had never done this before. I probably didn't need to do this, but for some reason, I followed along with the naked lady on the hanger.

It *all* feels lumpy and weird to me… I must not be doing it right. I did the same on the left side – it felt different. The lumpiness towards the top felt kinda hard - like a marble was stuck in there.

I shut the water off and grabbed the teal bath towel hanging over the shower rod. It's probably nothing – Mama or Crystal never had any problems with their breasts.

I quickly dried off and rubbed some cocoa butter on my ashy arms. I reached for my hot pink panties and oversized *Dope Moms Don't Sleep* T-shirt.

Was that really a l*ump, lump*? Was it really something to be worried about?... Probably not. I know breast problems run in families and Ma and Crystal were fine - I probably am too.

Too tired to think anymore, I dove underneath the flowered, purple comforter and sheets. As tired as I was, I couldn't go to sleep - I tossed and turned. Thoughts about school, work, and To-Do-Lists poured into my head from everywhere.

I glanced at the clock on the nightstand – if I go to sleep *right* now, I'll get four hours. Please Lord, help your child go to sleep! In Jesus name, Amen! I shut my eyes as tight as I could and prayed for my mind to shut off.

Com-Bustible

"Really?! Both of us could've made that light!", I yelled at the car in front of me.

Traffic lights never work in my favor! If I wanted the light to be red - to put on some lipstick, sign a permission slip, or send a text - they would *all* be green! But since I was running a little late this morning, every one of them was red!

I huffed and puffed - I could feel my nerves getting' bad about being late to work so, I called Mama to distract me.

"Good morning, Ma! What'cha been up to?"

From the depths of her soul, she gathered up the most sarcastic voice she could find and answered,

"Hell must be freezing over! Erica called her Mama on this bless-ed morning?!

"C'mon now Ma! You know I'm super busy with the boys, working full-time and pulling a full load this semester!"

I can't believe she was guilt-trippin' me like this! - I did need to do better though. It had been about a month since I heard her sarcastically, loving voice.

"Is everything alright?" You staying on top of everything?

– the bills, the boys, school?" she asked.

She was always worried about her baby girl.

"Oh yeah Mama, you know I always make it happen. I learned that from you - so it's all good!"

The lies I just told my Mama! God knows I wish she would get on the first available, bike, motorcycle, spaceship, *anything* and come take care all of us! My pride wouldn't let me tell her that the struggle was real!

"You know, I'm *just* a phone call away. You and my grandbabies are always welcome to come for a visit – however long you need," she said, reminding me she and her "friend" Mr. Eddie had moved to Florida a few months ago.

"I know Mama ... we should all get together for Thanksgiving! You can even invite that stuck- up first child of yours! I'll even sit by her and fake smile - I miss you *that* much Mama!"

"That would make me happier than a roach in a restaurant! All of us under the *same* roof, at the *same* table, laughing with each other – that would be my dream come true!", she said.

Truth be told, I could only picture myself *laughing at* Crystal's "proper talking accent" and her stomping out of the room with her nose pointed in the air - like she was some kind of special poodle- girl please!

"I guess Mama -", I replied not wanting to crush her dreams.

"Do you know if anyone in our family ever had problems with their breasts - like cancer?"

"Well, one of your aunties on your daddy's side had it – about fifteen years ago. I remember she was really involved with helping this women's group, uh... uh...Pink Crusaders! – Why?"

"Last night, I - I felt something, umm, kinda like a small marble in my left breast. I know I probably shouldn't be worried because I really don't know if I was doing the test right- it's probably noth---"

"Erica Divine Thomas! Stop talking crazy and go get tested - TODAY!", she said, cutting me off like a minivan dropping off five kids at three different schools.

"Mama, I – I, I can't call out of work! My supervisor gonna trip -like real hard!"

"Look, I don't care if he *trip, flip, and dip*! You tell your supervisor that *I said,* you can't come in today! Call the doctor as soon as we hang up!"

As soon as Mama's voice went sky high, I could feel my eyelashes getting damp- I pulled the car over.

"Yes, ma'am!", I was ugly crying now with my mouth wide open.

"Don't worry about that job or about *anything* else Erica. Take care of yourself Baby – do it for you *and* the boys. "Call me back, as soon as you make an appointment."

"Ok Mama … Love you, bye," I hung up the phone.

I dried my face with a *Chicken Charlies* napkin from the glove box and searched my phone for the women's imaging center – it was about fifteen minutes away from my job.

Once they ran my insurance, they scheduled to see me at noon. I called *Shoe Paradise* and just like I expected, Marcus was straight trippin'!

After I explained to him that my insurance wouldn't cover this if I didn't go today, he toned it down a bit, but not without saying,

"You know you'll have to make these hours up right? We need all hands on deck for the new displays and inventory."

I started to tell him what Mama said, but that would've gotten me fired. Instead I said,

"I'll be in first thing tomorrow and I will make up the hours before the week is out.

"Ok Erica, I'm counting on you to keep your word."

Bust Check

"You'll put your left breast on top of this surface here. This part will come down on top and take pictures," said the lady in pink scrubs.

"Is it gonna hurt?", I asked. I didn't like to be in pain- I paid my dues with childbirth.

"There's going to be some slight pressure and you may be a little uncomfortable, but it won't hurt," she replied.

I propped by C- cup on top of the surface like she told me to. My right foot wouldn't stop shaking as I watched the machine come down towards my breast.

"Oww, Shhhh!", I screamed staring at the lady as she turned the knobs – *Ms. Pink Scrubs* straight lied to me!

"Hold still ma'am. We just need a few more pictures and then we're done. "

I closed my eyes and prayed for this thing to be done. I don't know what I was expecting, but what I *wasn't* expecting was for my breast to get squished like a Cuban sandwich!

"All done!" she said, handing me a paper with instructions.

"So, I log onto this website to get my results?" I asked pointing to the white sheet.

"Yes, and your doctor will also get a copy of the results. It may take up to seventy-two hours before your results are posted to the portal.".

(Seventy-two hours? Who had that kind of time to find out if something was wrong with them?)

"Ok… thanks," I replied as she left the room for me to get dressed.

Bust-ed

I was on the sales floor helping *Big Foot* pick something out for her daughter's wedding when my phone buzzed against my thigh.

"Excuse me ma'am, I'll be back in just a minute," I said, walking towards the stockroom.

I didn't recognize the number, but I answered anyway,

"Hello?"

"This is Nurse Tammy from Dr. Shaffer's office. Is this Ms. Thomas?"

"Yes…", my heart dropped into my stomach.

"We have the results from the mammogram you had on yesterday. The doctor wants you to go over to the imaging center and have a biopsy done at 2 o'clock tomorrow."

"Why, wh-why do I need that?", I asked.

"It's a test that will let the doctor know if a spot that was seen on the mammogram is cancerous or not."

"Ok... A-at the same place I went to yesterday?"

"Yes. We have you scheduled to see Dr. Shaffer on next Wednesday at three-fifteen. Be sure to bring someone with you to both appointments," she answered.

"Everything gonna be fine E - I just know it is," Sheena said, hugging my arm as we walked into the exam room.

The room was freezing cold. I sat in the hard chair going back and forth between biting my nails and bouncing my knee like a basketball. This was worse than when I had that emergency C-section with Kev.

"Hello, how's everyone today?", Dr. Shaffer said as he as he closed the door behind him.

"Fine," we answered at the same time, anxious to hear the news.

"Good. When you had your mammogram done, there was an area of concern in the upper right quadrant of your left breast - right here," he pointed at the poster on the wall.

The more he talked the sweatier my hands got and the faster my leg shook – please don't let it be cancer, Lord please don't let it be cancer...

"We had you do the biopsy to determine if that area was cancerous. The results show that the lump is cancerous, but..."

"GOD NOOO! This can't be true, THIS CAN'T BE TRUE!", I shook my head and cried with Sheena's arms wrapped tightly around me.

"Ms. Thomas, treatment for breast cancer is *very* successful nowadays. Dr. Bowers is the best oncologist I know and he's going to come up with the best plan of action for you."

It was almost like someone hit the mute button on Dr. Shaffer as soon as he said the word, "cancer". All I could see was his mouth moving and feel my heart skipping like double-dutch.

When Dr. Shaffer left the room, I stared up at the white ceiling tiles with tears streaming down.

"Friend, don't chu worry! Imma be here for *whatever* you need! Everything is gonna be alright!", Sheena said as she held my hand and helped me stand to my feet.

While Sheena stood at the check- out window to get information about my oncology appointment, I sat in the crowded lobby with my thoughts...

Cancer?... At twenty-eight?... Like, how?! I will *not* leave my boys like this! - I'm all they have! This just ain't right, it ain't fair! -the tears started to fall again.

I was in such a daze over the devastating news that before I knew it, we were sitting in the parking lot of the boys' school. I could feel Sheena's eyes studying my face.

"E, are you ok?", she asked.

"I -I just don't know...I don't know what to do...I don't know what to say..."

"I've been working soooo hard Sheen! - You know I have! Trying to have better and do better for me and my boys...now this!"

"I know, you good to those boys and you'll keep being good to them. Imma make sure of that," Sheena said.

"Will you call my Mama for me?", I asked.

"Let's call her together. I'll put it on speakerphone."

I could feel my throat swelling up and my eyes start to blur.

"Hey Ms. Christine, this Sheena. Me and Erica just coming back from her appointment – she sitting right here, she can hear you."

"Erica… you ok baby?" Mama asked.

"It's cancer Mama! It's cancer!", I sobbed through the tears.

"Don't you worry about *nothing*! I'll be there by Friday morning and we'll beat this thing – *together*!

I can't explain it, hearing Mama say those words – her saying that she would be there for me, eased my fears. It soothed me the way the sound of rain hitting the concrete does. I was going to be ok – *we* were gonna be ok.

9 The Devoted Woman

Come hell or high water, rain or shine, the Devoted Woman is going to Make. It. Happen. When life throws everything at her *plus* the kitchen sink, she won't fold. The Devoted Woman willfully sacrifices herself for the people or things that are most important to her. She's a "Go-getter" who won't let anything stand in the way of accomplishing a goal, fulfilling a dream, or executing her vision - not even herself.

Even when she fails or is let down by others, time after time, she finds the strength to bounce back and move forward from *any* situation. With the Cape of Commitment propelling her forward, she will juggle and struggle to make it happen.

When the Devoted Woman makes a commitment, she will sacrifice everything within her to love it, nurture it, and support it. This can cause her to develop "tunnel-vision" on whatever it is she is striving to achieve. On the inside, she may wish, hope, and pray for someone to help her, but her pride won't allow her to ask.

You can find the Devoted Woman in several walks of life, but single mothers are often spotted wearing this cape. Single mothers are some of the most devoted people to ever walk the face of this Earth. Don't get me wrong, most mothers sacrifice and give their everything to their children, but often times, single mothers do it alone.

The Devoted Woman's commitments often overshadow her individual wants and needs. Her dreams and visions are usually tied to someone else's wellbeing or happiness. This can lead to a decline in physical and mental health.

She often works harder and longer than everyone else on the team. As a result, she can become disappointed and frustrated when others don't commit themselves with the same intensity as she does. Without thinking twice, the Devoted Woman gives herself away to her commitments. Even if others fold, she will be the last woman standing.

It would be great if the Devoted Woman applied her unwavering dedication to her health. However, she usually spreads herself too thin to make a long-term commitment that would improve her health status. However, it can be difficult for the Devoted Woman to see her health as beneficial to those she is committed to. The Devoted Woman is a very accomplished woman, but unfortunately her health often comes last in the race.

The Healthy Truth About Erica

Erica burned the candle at both ends, trying to stay afloat financially and maintain emotional and physical presence with her sons. There's no doubt that Erica was devoted to all things Kev and Kenny, but she had forgotten to be devoted to the most important person in her life and theirs – Erica.

Erica's tendency to fully devote herself to her dreams and visions didn't just start when she became a mother. At a young age, Erica's dream and vision was to have a family with Kennon. She was his "ride-or-die chick", willing to struggle and endure physical, verbal, and emotional abuse, all in the name of love and devotion.

Erica defined love as remaining loyal to a person, no matter what. When her last son was born, Erica's loyalty and commitment fully shifted towards motherhood. Although she loved Kennon and wanted that happy family, she wasn't willing to die trying to make it happen.

As a result, Erica became laser-focused on doing whatever was necessary to provide the life that her boys deserved. She wouldn't allow herself to ask for help from others or let them know she was struggling. She wanted to prove to herself and others that she was making a comeback from the naive teenaged mother she once was.

To say that she had a full plate is an understatement – her plate runneth over! She worked a full-time job that she hated, went to school full-time, took care of the house, was a football mom, and even had a hair braiding side hustle on the weekend - Whew!

With so much focus and commitment on others and achieving goals, it's easy for diseases like breast cancer to sneak up on a Devoted Woman. Erica gave the best of herself to her children, while leaving herself on the back burner, scorched and burned.

It had been a few years since Erica saw a doctor for anything. No matter if it was her head, heart, or hand, she would grab some over-the-counter medicine and keep it moving.

A cough, a headache, or a fever was never a good enough reason to call out of work. Calling out of single motherhood just wasn't an option -there are no sick days. Even when Erica thought that something was seriously wrong, she tried talking herself out of it.

Breast cancer is the most common cancer found in women world-wide and the second most common cancer in American women. The best forms of prevention are screenings like the self-breast exam (SBE) or with imaging like a mammogram or an ultrasound.

Before that night in the shower, Erica had never done an SBE, which made her uncertain of what her hands were feeling. An SBE should be done monthly, about seven to ten days after your period, when your breasts are less tender and lumpy. If you are in menopause, the SBE should be done on the same day of every month (7).

Monthly SBEs help you become familiar with your breasts and makes it more likely for you to notice if something isn't normal. Young women and girls can do this exam, too! You can make notes to describe what your breasts feel and look like (lumpy on the top left, smaller on the right) when you examine them. This way, you can compare one month to the next.

Current research states that there is little evidence that an SBE or a clinical breast exam (one done by a health professional) help find breast cancer when a women gets a screening mammogram. From my experience, an SBE helped my mother detect her breast cancer. So I say, "Get to know your breasts!"

If you do feel or see something that isn't quite right, you should schedule to see your doctor. Your doctor will perform a breast exam and may order a mammogram or an ultrasound to determine if cancer is present.

Not only was Erica not aware of her own health, she had no idea about the health conditions in her family tree. Having a first-degree relative (mother, daughter sister) or multiple second- degree relatives (aunts, nieces, grandmother) affected by breast cancer increases your risk for breast cancer (8). We have no control over our family health history and the following risk factors are beyond our   control as   well:

Being born female (#1 risk factor)

Getting older

Dense breast tissue

Getting your period before 12 years old

Radiation to the chest

Being diagnosed with cancer in the past

Prescribed use of hormone replacement therapy

BRCA1 or BRCA2 genetic mutations

Although Erica had quit smoking years ago, she still put herself at risk for breast cancer. Every day, we must fight against the temptation of making unhealthy lifestyle choices. Sometimes it feels overwhelming to live a healthy lifestyle, but it can be done! – One healthy choice at a time! Some unhealthy risk factors for breast cancer are:

Smoking

Drinking alcohol

The use of birth control pills

Not managing your stress levels

Obesity

Erica is only twenty-eight years old, she never imagined that she would be diagnosed with breast cancer. A woman being diagnosed with breast cancer in her twenties and thirties is relatively rare. These diagnoses only make up five percent of breast cancer cases. When women under the age of forty are diagnosed, they usually have more complicated cases.

Knowing your family history is so important! It can prompt you to have a conversation with your doctor about getting your mammogram before forty-five years old (the recommended age for women who have an average risk) or genetic testing for the BRCA1 or BRCA2 genes. Having the proper screenings and testing can help you save your life.

10 Don't Forget About YOU!

There's a good chance that we've never met, but I'm willing to bet that you have a calendar of some sort. That calendar is filled with color-coded events like, "Kid's Appointment", "Payment Due", or "Work Deadline". Where is the event that says, "Me Time"? If you're reading this book, there's a good chance that the "Me Time" event rarely happens if at all.

When it comes to motherhood, marriage, friendship, and teamwork on the job, you're all in! It's ok to be "all-in", but it's not ok to neglect caring for yourself in the process. I know, I know, your calendar and schedule are already loaded. Adding one more thing seems to be impossible and you can't seem to figure out how to carve out a little time for you.

The solution to this is simple – Make it happen! I don't mean you saying, "Yeah, I'm going to start back singing with the group again" or "One day, I'll get back to doing that". When I say, "Make it happen", that means that you don't cancel on yourself because of something or someone else. You may have to *reschedule* yourself, but don't make it a habit.

Putting "You" on your To-Do list and the things that bring you joy, peace, and restoration is necessary for good health and wellness. Let's be real. We both know that the stuff on the bottom of the To-Do List doesn't get done that day- sometimes not even that month! Put yourself at the top of the To-Do list!

Take thirty minutes every day to do something solely for yourself. It can be something simple like going for a walk, journaling, watching a TV show, reading a book, or just sitting in silence alone. A simple thirty minutes every day adds up to three and a half hours every week!

Try choosing a time of day when the rest of your world is quiet (kids are asleep or before work), it will help you be consistent in caring for yourself. This will also help you get rid of those feelings and thoughts of guilt that sound like, "I should really be cleaning my house instead of doing this." Consistently putting yourself on your schedule will give you more energy to tackle the other things on your To-Do List.

A schedule without love, commitment, and care for yourself can be the fire that burns your mental, emotional, and physical health to the ground! In other words, it's not optional! When you're surrounded by people that greatly depend on you, it is a must that you set aside the time to love on you! – No excuses!

While you're penciling in your self-care time, it's a good idea to schedule important health screenings and appointments in advance. It's helpful to put these appointments on a physical or digital calendar so you won't forget them.

When you forget your appointments, you run the risk of having your appointment rescheduled months down the road. The problem with this is, if your body is suffering from a progressive disease that you aren't aware of, like breast cancer, this can delay detection and treatment. In worse cases, your condition can reach a point that is beyond treatment.

Don't let the fact that you feel "just fine" hinder you from making and keeping your doctor's appointments. You must keep in mind that not all diseases have noticeable signs or symptoms. Sometimes, it's a result from routine bloodwork that leads your doctor to finding an underlying condition or disease.

Keeping all of your annual screenings and appointments around the same time each year will help you remember these important dates. It will help establish a routine in your schedule and you will be less likely to schedule other events during this time.

If you don't have a primary care provider, start doing your research to get one. A good place to start is by calling your insurance provider to find out which doctors in your area accept your insurance. It's a good idea to get the names of a few doctors who may be farther away from you as well, just so you have more options.

Before you make an appointment, please do your research! Is the front desk receptionist nice or nasty? Do they charge extra for certain procedures? Save yourself the time and money by reading online reviews and talking to other women who are patients at this office.

When you find a doctor you're interested in, call the office just to ask some general questions like: "Are you accepting new patients?" or "What are the steps to become a new patient?"

Make note of how helpful (or not) the receptionist is. A good or bad receptionist can be the difference between life and death, literally. The receptionist will be your first point of contact to make appointments, get prescriptions, or a referral to another doctor.

Call around to doctor's offices during the months of open enrollment. Doctors are usually accepting new patients during this time. This will help you schedule the appointments you need for screenings in the upcoming calendar year.

Some women skip out on having important screenings, like mammograms, because they simply can't afford the out-of-pocket cost. This is not a reason to forgo what you need to take care of yourself. If you don't have insurance or if you are underinsured, you can contact your local American Cancer Society, county health department, or search for other non-profit organizations that assist with mammograms.

When it comes to the people you love and things you want to accomplish in your life, you are relentlessly devoted. Now it's time to invest those superpowers into you living the healthiest version of your life! You deserve it!

11 The Perfect Picture

My eyelids flew open at three-fifteen in the morning. My heart raced as I lied there in warm, wet sheets.

"NOOOO!", I screamed so loud that Chris sprang up from the bed sheets.

"What's wrong babe?!", he asked, reaching for the lamp on the nightstand.

I couldn't speak ... but I didn't have to. He could see the blood-stained sheets and he knew, just like I did, we had lost the baby.... that was five months ago.

The tile floor felt like ice underneath me. I sat with my back against the closed bathroom door, my knees tucked underneath my chin. I really wasn't in the Christmas spirit. I especially wasn't looking forward to being around my family, asking me a million and one questions about my life.

"Babe, everything ok in there?", Chris asked through the locked, white painted door.

"Yeah, I'm just, you know - getting my hair together," I answered.

"Ok, I'll be in the living room watching the game. I'm ready when you are," Chris said as he walked away.

Who was I kidding? I hadn't even taken the satin bonnet off my head! I didn't want Chris to know I had taken another pregnancy test. He didn't want me obsessing over getting pregnant, but I *needed* for this test to be positive!

I felt like I was disappointing him every time a test said I wasn't pregnant. Three years ago, we had our dream wedding at my family's church - it was pure perfection!

The reception was THEE absolute best I've ever seen! A six-tiered, classic vanilla cake, covered in rose gold fondant, a live band and DJ, an ice sculpture, and an open bar! We both landed good jobs and bought a house in the suburbs. Everything was going according to plan - except for this.

By now, there should've been a chubby toddler on the other side of this bathroom door trying to break in yelling, "Mommy, open door!" - but there wasn't.

We had just started trying "on purpose" a few months ago. I just didn't understand why the tests always came up negative –I was using an ovulation kit and a fertility app.

More than twenty minutes had passed - I knew the test was ready, but I wasn't. I tip-toed across the floor and towards the countertop like I was about to steal fine jewelry. As I got closer, I squeezed my eyes shut.

I stood there peeking through my lashes before fully

opening my eyes - just one blue line. I picked up the test to see if there was a faint line hiding in the background – nope. Not pregnant - again.

I snatched the bonnet from my head and stared in the mirror through my tear-glazed eyes. What's wrong with me? Chris is a good man! He deserves to be a father! Why can't I do what a woman is naturally *supposed* to do? I'm such a failure...

I bottled my feelings and blotted my eyes. I brushed my face with spicy brown foundation and lined my eyes with midnight eyeliner. I was careful to not get the Merry Merlot lipstick on my teeth. I ran my fingers over every braid, checking for fly-away strands, before wrapping them into a neat bun on top of my head. I looked perfect.

Perfectly Hidden

"Heyyyy, my favorite cousin!", Tony came to the door with his arms opened wide. He said that to *everybody* – hoping they would "loan" him fifty dollars by the time we finished dinner.

I gave him a quick side-hug and spoke to everyone sitting in the living room. I went straight for the kitchen in hopes of finding my mom. There she was, putting the finishing touches on the honey baked ham.

"It smells so good in here Mom! - like Martha Stewart lives here or something!", I said.

"Awww, that's so sweet of you to say! Glad you're here Michelle", she said giving me the biggest hug.

"Chris come with you?"

"Yes, he's in there watching the game. Hopefully, Uncle Melvin isn't giving him too much of a hard time,".

"O good! I wouldn't want Christmas dinner without my favorite son-in-law sitting at the table!", she said.

"Mom, you always work so hard on this – ham, turkey, fresh rolls, the whole nine. You should start having us bring covered dishes you know?"

"O heavens no! Your aunties would just burn up the cornbread and the sweet potato pies! I want this to be perfect! – and if you want perfection, you have to do it yourself!", she said while covering the dessert table with a white lace tablecloth.

"Well, you got a point there... Where's Daddy?"

"He should be bringing the fried turkey in from the back in a minute now.

I peeked through the beige kitchen curtains to see if I could spot him. All I could see was four of Daddy's old buddies talking smack and playing spades at the card table. There was no way I was walking into that war zone.

I turned my attention to Mom who was thoughtfully placing the desserts on the table. I gave her a hand with the three pecan pies, four sweet potato pies, three red velvet cakes, double fudge brownies, and two platters of sugar cookies shaped like Christmas trees, reindeer, and snowmen on the table.

"SHELLY PIE!", dad shouted as he burst into the kitchen with a twenty-five-pound turkey in tow.

"Hi daddy! Mom told me you were outside, but I wasn't

about to risk Mr. Bobby asking me to set him up with one of my friends!"

"That old knucklehead!", he laughed. Did you bring Chris with you?"

"Yes sir, he's in there with your brother...you may need to rescue him."

"We'll all be stuffing our bellies full in about ten minutes - he won't have to suffer much longer!", Dad assured me as he placed the turkey on the dining room table.

The adults sat at two conjoined tables in the formal dining room while the kids took their seats at a cute little white table with a Mr. and Mrs. Claus centerpiece.

Twenty-seven of us gathered around the massive tables adorned with gold chargers, red cloth napkins, and a nativity scene centerpiece – it was better than perfect! We all held hands, bowed our heads as Daddy said the prayer and blessing. As soon as we all said, "Amen!" Aunt Rose set her sights on me.

"Chelle, when are you and Chris going to give my sister some grandbabies? You know, she and your daddy are getting older by the second!"

"I'm not *that* old, BUT I sure wouldn't mind spoiling those sweet babies with toys and cookies," Mom said.

"I really thought you were pregnant right now - seeing as how your hips have spread and your stomach is a little pudgy," Aunt Rose said, pointing at my burgundy sweater.

Everyone had their forks in their mouths and their eyes glued to me... this is *exactly* why I hated big family gatherings!

I hadn't told anyone, not even my Mom, about the miscarriage.

I didn't even want them knowing that Chris and I were trying. The questions would rush in like a flood – questions that I didn't know the answers to or just didn't want to talk about.

I responded, "Well, we're trying to get settled in our careers before we start our family - we're just being responsible."

Aunt Rose said, "You've been working at that bank for a looong time and I know Chris making good money at his job – what ya'll waiting for? Jesus to come back?"

She didn't fall for my excuse...I didn't know what else to say – this embarrassing questionnaire was never going to be over...

"She waiting on you to get out of her bizness! -*that's* what she waiting on!", Daddy said, he could feel my irritation radiating across the dinner table.

"Raymond, nobody was talking to you! I was just asking *my niece* about something! – OK?!", said Aunt Rose.

"Shelly can have *zero* babies or *twenty* babies - it's all up to her and Chris! She doesn't have to get your approval on *when* to have them, *Nosy Rosy!*", Daddy said.

Aunt Rose flung her hand across her chest as if she were clutching some imaginary pearls and stared at Mom. Mom sipped her iced tea and gave her a look that said, "You better shut up before Raymond puts you out of here!"

Sensing the tension Chris asked, "Mr. Raymond, who do you have your money on this year for the Super Bowl?"

As the men quoted football stats and recapped the season, I started to think on the fact that I was the only one there who didn't have any children. No matter how much I talked about the other things going on in my life like work, the projects I was doing with my sorority, or trips with Chris, nothing seemed to distract them from the fact that I was childless.

Aunt Rose never caught the hint that the conversation made me uncomfortable – or maybe she didn't care. I sat amongst the chatter, spreading the cornbread dressing around with my fork – my appetite had vanished.

"Michelle, come into the kitchen and help me bring out the desserts," my mom said.

I took the napkin from my lap, laid it on the table and followed her.

"Are you ok Michelle?", mom asked.

"I'm ok – it's just that I don't like talking about certain things in front of the whole family. Aunt Rose is always on me about having kids. She doesn't know what is going on so she shouldn't keep badgering me!"

"Just ignore her honey. She likes getting into everyone's business. Can you believe your daddy called her Nosy Rosy?! -I could've just flew out of my chair!

I laughed so hard until I felt some relief. Mom had a way of lightening the mood and keeping family members from throwing punches.

"When you and Chris are ready, you will have the perfect little children and you'll be a perfect little mother."

"Thanks Mom."

We ate our dessert around the Christmas tree and watched the kids tear open their gifts. Chris cleared the ripped wrapping paper and boxes from the hardwood floor while I helped Mom put away the leftovers and dishes. After what seemed like the longest visit ever, we said our goodbyes and headed to the car.

"Are you ok? Your Aunt was way out of line, trying to be up in our business like that," Chris said as he buckled his seatbelt.

"I – I'm used to her being like that...", I answered, even though my heart felt like the shreds of Christmas paper that covered my parent's floor.

"You may be used to it, but she needs to chill and stay out of our business!"

"I'm ok baby. Thanks for checking on me," I said while reapplying the Merry Merlot in the mirrored visor.

He held my hand as I looked through the windows at the strings of lights all over the city. All I could do was think about the pool of blood and the "negative" test from earlier today.

Between my thoughts, I glanced over at him and smiled, hoping that my face told a different story than my head and heart. I didn't want him knowing... knowing that I felt useless to him as a wife and that he deserved so much more.

Painfully Pictured

"Just sign here and we'll start the process for your car loan," I said to the newlywed couple sitting on the other side of my desk.

Mrs. Johnson looked at her husband with smiling eyes and excitement about purchasing their first car together since they tied the knot.

It was moments like this that made me love what I did as a loan officer. Everyday didn't give me a warm, tingly feeling, but I knew I was making a difference.

This moment would've been more enjoyable if it wasn't for "Aunt Flow". It felt like my pelvis was on fire and my back was aching so terribly bad. I just hated being at work with these brutal cramps!

I felt anxious about getting the Johnsons out of here so I could hurry to the ladies' room and change my tampon. It had only been about forty-five minutes since the last change, but "Aunt Flow" didn't care. Every month, she was getting heavier and more painful – she was ruthless!

The medicine I took a few hours ago wasn't helping at all. Maybe I should just go home early... no, then they would probably give David that Senior Loan Officer promotion over me. At least the vomiting and diarrhea episode of the "Attack of Aunt Flow" happened over the weekend.

I was wearing the *Flowology* Super Plus tampons along with the super plus pad for backup - just in case I couldn't make it to change in time. I couldn't wait to get home to hot cup of green tea, a heating pad, and a cozy blanket.

At least then I wouldn't have to be paranoid about staining my navy-blue trousers or wonder if people could tell I had on this "baby diaper" - Come on four o'clock!

It felt good to be home in my gray sweats and fuzzy socks. I propped my feet up on the couch and pressed my low back into toasty heating pad. I strolled through my timeline - three-hundred and thirty-three "Likes" on our holiday pictures. We looked like the perfect couple in our Christmas PJs.

"CHRIS, CAN YOU BRING MY RED BLANKET FROM THE BEDROOM?", I hollered out towards the man cave.

"ALRIGHT BABE!", he yelled back.

He was extra sweet to me when "Aunt Flow" was in town. He had *some* idea about my discomfort, but he didn't know how agonizing the pain was for me – I never told him.

"Need anything else?", he asked as he threw the blanket over my legs

"Nope. I'm starting dinner in a few minutes. Is chicken alfredo and spinach salad ok?"

"I'm starvin' like Marvin, Michael, *and* Melvin! I'll eat anything! - if you season it right!", he chuckled

"You know what, speaking of Melvin, I should call Uncle Melvin and have him bring one of those squirrels over for dinner! You know, he keeps some in his deep freezer year-round! Squirrel alfredo it is!"

"Baby, please don't feed me that countrified chicken! My little city boy stomach wouldn't be able to take it! - it's basically roadkill!"

"Alright, alright, I'll spare you this time! You can go back to your Man Hive – Cave or whatever you call it," I said as he scurried back to his seventy - inch T.V. and surround sound.

My stomach was hurting so bad! I didn't feel like boiling a pot of water - I shouldn't have told Chris I was making dinner. I didn't want to disappoint him though. He deserved a wife who cooked him a hot meal, at least four times a week.

I scrolled my timeline a little more hoping that my stomach would settle before I started dinner. I came across this post from Tracy Gaines, a girl that I went to my high school:

"It's a cold world out here ya'll ... After five years of working my fingers to the bone for these sorry M'Fers at Brenton Law, they fired me! Really?! REALLY?! Who does that to a single mother with three kids? They said I missed too many days - they knew about my female problems when I first started! I can't help that some days I couldn't get out of the bed to come in, but I always made up my work! Loyalty just don't exist out there ya'll...

She was beyond pissed and I don't blame her! That's exactly why I try not to miss work *or* leave early. The higher ups will take it out on you for not being there every minute – even if you are sick.

I scanned through some of the comments and one from Harmony Love caught my attention:

"I'm so sorry this happened to you Sis. Please find a good GYN! This doesn't sound normal! It could be something serious causing you to miss that many days.

I never thought about it like that... several days of painful cramps, heavy bleeding, diarrhea, and vomiting was always my norm. I got my period at thirteen and it just got worse over time.

My mom told me it was a normal part of being a woman. It was that way for her, too until after she had me.

She taught me which medicines to take to help with the pain and the best time to use tampons, pads, or a combination of both. I remember in high school, I would miss two, sometimes three days from school. Now, I just deal with it because I don't want to lose my job or put too much strain on Chris.

I go for my Pap every year, but I never talk about these horrible cramps and heavy bleeding – it's normal. The last time I went to my OBGYN was to talk about the D&C procedure and for a follow-up after the miscarriage.

I wonder if my horrible periods have something to with me not getting pregnant and staying pregnant... Maybe I should take Harmony Love's advice and go see a different gynecologist.

Perfect Health

"MICHELLE MORGAN," the nurse called me back into the exam room. I picked up my purse, put the *Women Today* magazine onto the plastic rack, and flashed the nurse a smile as I approached her.

I'm glad the bank was closed for MLK day so I wouldn't have to miss work for this appointment.

"Remove everything from the bottom and put this on facing forward." She handed me the paper gown and said,

"There's a drape to put over your lap on the exam table. Dr. Givens will be in with you shortly." The blond-haired nurse shut the door behind her before I could even ask her name.

I sat on black vinyl chair in the corner of the exam room. As I unzipped my brown leather boots, I hoped that Dr. Givens had better bedside manner than her nurse. If not, I may as well pack my goodies up and go!

I tucked my panties between the folded stack I had made with my jeans and sweater. I sat on the stiff white paper lining the exam table as my sock-covered feet dangled below. As I slipped the paper gown over my black bra, I prayed that Dr. Givens really was "The Best in Richmond" like the reviews had said.

"Hi, Mrs. Morgan! I'm Dr. Givens!" I've reviewed your paperwork, but I'd like to hear from you as to why you're here to see me today.

Dr. Givens was a breath of fresh air! Her dark brown hair perfectly framed her wide brown eyes and her teeth were as white as the Virginia snow.

Her eyes were so inviting that as I started to speak, the tears began to flow as I responded,

"My husband and I have been trying to have a baby for a while now. Back in July, I had a miscarriage... something I read pushed me to come talk to you about how painful my periods are – it's been that way since they started.

"I'm so sorry to hear about what you've experienced," she said, handing me a tissue from the pink paisley box.

"I'm going to do a pelvic exam today, so I can get some more information on what's going on with your body – is that ok?"

I nodded, "Yes" as I crumpled the damp tissue in my fist.

"Ok, let's slide your hips all the way down to the edge of the table and put your feet in the stirrups," she calmly instructed.

I hated having this done - it always hurt. I took deep breathes as Dr. Givens pressed on my stomach and examined my cervix.

"None of what I'm doing should be painful, maybe a little uncomfortable, but not painful," she said.

"*Everything* you're doing is painful - it always hurts," I responded.

"Does it hurt when you have a bowel movement or during sex with your husband?", she asked while removing her gloves.

"I – sometimes it feels ok… it can be uncomfortable at times, but it's normal," I replied.

"My next steps are to order a pelvic ultrasound and possibly a procedure called a laparoscopy to determine if you have any reproductive conditions."

"That kind of pain, during your periods and intercourse, is NOT normal. In the meantime, I'm going to prescribe you something for pain while we get to the bottom of this. Don't hesitate to call my office if you have questions," she said while laying her hand onto mine.

I tossed the paper gown into the trash and was a bit dumbfounded – all this time, my *normal* pain was NOT normal! I exercise, I eat healthy, I always take care of myself. I couldn't believe that something more could be happening! I work so hard for things to be perfect for me and Chris! We deserve to have our family!

Perfectly Imperfect

"I'm going out to the car!", I yelled towards the bedroom where Chris was closing the white faux wood blinds.

The still coldness of the black interior was a perfect match for my mood. How could I have let this happen? I should have done more to take care of myself – now we might never be able have a baby!

"You got everything you need Babe?", asked Chris as he closed the driver side door.

"I have everything… I really don't want to do this surgery. This is *not* the way things were supposed to happen for us! We were already supposed to have a child by now!"

"I believe we'll have a child – correction, we will have children! - I just know that we will," Chris said.

"That's easy for you to say! Your body is not the one that's malfunctioning!"

"Chris, I'm sorry I yelled. This - this is all my fault and I've brought you into this mess!", I bawled like a baby.

"Mess? You and the word "mess" don't even belong in the same sentence! I remember watching your long, brown legs strut across the lawn at the Rhythm and Rhymes Festival."

"My eyes followed you all the way to your seat because I didn't want to lose sight of you." Five years later and I still don't want to take my eyes off you. Our life may not be perfect, but you are the perfect woman for me. We're in this together - that's all that matters."

His voice was as smooth as the music that played the day we met. "Chris, how could I not know?! All of the pain - pain in my back, in my pelvis, low energy, cramping… pain when we make love," I whispered. Chris' eyebrows looked as if they would meet in the middle.

"Babe, you never told me any of this…why would you not tell me?"

"I was ashamed, ashamed that I wouldn't measure up to be the wife that you deserved. Telling you about my pain would make me look weak or like I'm not cut out to be everything you want me to be," I responded.

"I didn't marry you to *be* my everything, I married you because you *are* my everything. Let me do what I was made to do, let me be your leaning post. It doesn't matter what it is, I will be there for you, but I can't if you don't tell me."

My princess cut diamond seemed to sparkle brighter than ever as he raised my hand to his smooth, soft lips. The guilt and shame of my imperfections started to melt away.

The truth was, I was tired…tired of beating myself up, tired of carrying this burden of pain, tired of trying to be a trophy wife when all my husband wanted was me, with all my flaws... and endometriosis, too.

12 The Perfect Woman

Perfect Paula. Flawless Florence. You've met her. Maybe she's your boss, your teacher from second grade, or maybe you see her staring at you from the other side of the mirror every morning. The Perfect Woman makes sure every strand of hair is perfectly placed and she's ever so careful to *never* make a mistake. If you point out a misspelled word or give a suggestion on how she can improve, she may not take it too well.

She's got the lakefront house, with the three-car garage, five doctoral degrees, but guess what? The Perfect Woman's successes are not enough for to let her guard down to imperfection. It's not uncommon for the Perfect Woman to set Washington Monument -sized goals and beat herself up if she doesn't achieve them according to schedule.

The Perfect Woman is usually pleasant and cordial, but can seem very stand-offish. She usually avoids opening up to people, even loved ones, about her fears or failures. Consequently, she may ax you from her life before letting you get close enough to discover anything about her that's less than perfect.

Not only does The Perfect Woman want to *be perfect*, she wants to be seen as perfect. She may never let you see her sweat, figuratively or literally, but internally, she fights a constant battle to maintain perfection. The Perfect Women sees personal problems or issues as threat to her perfectionism. If something threatens to tarnish her perfect image, she may downplay it, ignore it altogether, or commit emotional suicide over the death of her perfect image.

When things are an upside-down, inside-out mess, the Perfect Woman will find a way to conceal every blemish to maintain her perfect image. The Cape of Perfection can lead to her being dismissive of what's going on in reality.

The Cape of Perfection may have been introduced to the Perfect Woman's when she was just a little girl. She may have been under the constant pressure of high expectations to perform well academically, athletically, and be a be a socialite.

She may have put on the Cape of Perfection to avoid facing a flaw or as a tool to recover from a major setback. When she pretends that everything is "just perfect", she lies to herself and the people around her.

Even the best athlete can miss a shot, but it's difficult for the Perfect Woman to accept any misses in life. Deep down, The Perfect Woman knows that perfection is impossible, but every morning, she puts on that Cape of Perfection and heads out into the world.

It's a great practice for women to put the best version of themselves forward. However, when the Perfect Woman deceives herself about being perfect, it can lead to her overlooking what's happening in reality. That false sense of perfectionism can lead to the denial of something that is detrimental to her health and well-being.

The Healthy Truth About Michelle

Somewhere along life's journey, Michelle picked up the idea her that life must be picture-perfect, no exceptions. The Cape of Perfection looks gorgeous on the outside. It sparkles and shines when the light hits it, but inside, it's lined with wool that is hot, heavy, and itches like crazy.

No one on this Earth is perfect. Even if you strive for perfection, you will never achieve it – and that's ok. But in the Palace of Perfectionism, being perfect is the only way to be. Michelle's desire to keep up appearances at home and at work lead to her denying that something "imperfect" could be happening concerning her reproductive health.

Some of us are trained on how to be perfect from the time we are born with rules like, "Don't cross your legs at the knee" or "Don't smile too big, you'll get wrinkles". When it comes to dealing with the pain of our menstrual cycles we're taught "It's just a part of being a woman". Well, I'm here to tell you that a 20 out of 10 pain level is not a normal part of womanhood.

Michelle's menstrual cycle had been excruciatingly painful since it began at thirteen years old. The solution her mother gave her was to take pain meds, double up pads and tampons, and drink some hot tea. In her mom's defense, this was probably the same remedy her mother or doctor had given her while assuring her, "It's just a part of being a woman."

This dismissive way of thinking coupled with the Cape of Perfection can lead to ignoring the signs and symptoms associated with conditions like endometriosis. Michelle suffered in silence about the pain she endured regarding her reproductive health.

Her commitment to maintain a perfect image wouldn't allow her to take time off from work, discuss her feelings with her husband, or tell her mom about her miscarriage.

What exactly is endometriosis? Endometriosis is a condition that can affect the uterus and other organs of the body. So, what happens exactly? The exact cause of endometriosis is not quite understood but, there are a few theories that suggest what happens.

During a normal menstrual cycle, the lining of your uterus (endometrium) sheds and exits your body. With endometriosis, one theory suggests that *some* of the uterine lining attaches to other parts of the body like the ovaries, fallopian tubes, pelvis, and bladder. In rare cases, the lining can even reach as high as the lungs!

The lining, no matter where it's attached, can grow, bleed, and react to hormonal changes that occur during any part of the menstrual cycle. This is the retrograde menstruation theory. As you can imagine, this can cause debilitating pain. It is not a normal process and therefore, the pain that comes along with it is not normal either (9). Women with endometriosis can experience the following:

Excruciating menstrual cramps that can worsen

 Severe low back pain during, before, and after your period

 Pain during sex

 Pain with bowel movements and urination

 Heavy bleeding and long lasting cycles

 Changes in appetite or weight changes

Diarrhea and vomiting during your period

 Severe abdominal pain

How will you know if you have endometriosis? The first step is to be open with yourself about the pain you are *really* experiencing. Sometimes it's difficult to put a number on the pain you're experiencing, especially when you're a cape-wearing woman.

A better way to gauge your pain is to take note on how the pain affects your life. Have you quit doing activities you enjoy because of your pain? Are you taking more medication than usual? Are you spending most of your day in bed?

Once you've acknowledged to yourself that your pain is negatively impacting your life, it's time to talk to your doctor. Michelle would not have gotten to the bottom of what was causing her pain had she not selected a doctor who was willing and equipped to help her. Keep track of your symptoms in a health journal and take it with you to your appointments.

Be open and upfront with your doctor about the symptoms that you are experiencing. Remember, your doctors work for you! - not the other way around! If your doctor won't listen to you, find a new one to hand over your hard-earned coins to! You deserve it and your health depends on it!

Your doctor may then order a pelvic ultrasound to check for ovarian cysts, fibroids, or other conditions that may be causing your pain. The only way to diagnose endometriosis is via laparoscopy (surgical procedure using a laparoscope through small incisions). This procedure allows the doctor to see if the uterine lining is present outside of the uterus. The doctor will take a biopsy of the tissue and in some cases, the doctor will remove any lesions that are present.

Many women who suffer with endometriosis don't discover it until they begin struggling with infertility. A diagnosis with endometriosis does not guarantee that a woman will have difficulty getting pregnant or struggle with miscarriages. However, if reproductive organs are damaged from severe endometriosis or if hormones decrease the quality of eggs released, the chances of infertility increase.

Having severe pain from endometriosis does not equal to having severe damage nor does mild pain indicate a mild case. The only way to access the severity of endometriosis is by laparoscopic surgery. Some doctors will remove some the painful lesions during the surgery used to diagnosis endometriosis.

It's important for women with endometriosis to be in touch with how they are feeling so that those around them can assist them when it's needed. There's nothing to be ashamed of when it comes to the symptoms of endometriosis. Having a good support system can help you live a fulfilling life, even with endometriosis!

13 You're NOT Perfect!

Why do you feel the need to be perfect at all times and in all places? The truth is, you will *never* be perfect. You may make the world's most perfect pancakes, but the pancake batter probably runs down the sides of the bowl. – Perfection just doesn't exist!

I'm not saying that you shouldn't *strive* for perfection, but it's just not attainable. Say you wanted to lose one hundred pounds this month with exercise and diet. You can strive for this one-month goal, but it's just not attainable.

When you set a goal of perfection, what you end up achieving is disappointment and frustration. The Cape of Perfection shifts your focus to your mistakes and failures rather than your progress and triumphs. Perfectionism will cause you to overlook the fact that you lost eight pounds in one month and focus on the one-hundred pounds you didn't lose.

You may be asking, "Why even bother to strive for perfection if I'll never be perfect?" Instead of striving for perfection, strive to be the best version of yourself. You'll get close to perfection without experiencing the let-down of imperfection.

In my journey as a Christian, I strive to be like Jesus, but I know I'll never be Him. In other words, you won't get to watch the concert from the stage, but a front row seat will get you close – and that's great!

As women, we should strive for perfection in the things that are meaningful to us, but with this disclaimer in mind:

Perfection will not be obtained, but a favorable result is highly likely

When you stop trying to live in a perfect world, you will begin to appreciate all the things about you that are great. You will learn to embrace your imperfections rather than denying that you have room to grow. Your self-esteem and value will begin to blossom when you give yourself permission to be imperfect.

Not only will removing the Cape of Perfection improve your self-esteem, it will help to strengthen your relationships. Removing the cape allows those that love you an avenue to travel to your heart and emotions. I'm not saying to be vulnerable with everyone, but believe it or not, there are a few people who are waiting for the opportunity to be there for you, if you let them.

If you aren't exactly ready to let the world know that you aren't perfect, you can expose yourself on the pages of a journal. Journaling will allow you to say exactly how you feel without worrying about what someone is going to say about it. If you can't journal every day, a few times a week is a great start to removing the Cape of Perfection.

You can answer questions like, "How do I *really* feel?" or "What am I fearful of today?". Taking up a new hobby or interest is another good way to break down the illusion of perfection. If you've never decorated a cake before, more than likely you are going to make a mistake... or two...or three. Exposing yourself to activities or situations where you know you won't be perfect will help you toss the Cape of Perfection.

14 Work Hard, Play Hardly

"WAAA! A WAAAA! WAAA!", came screeching through the baby monitor. Two-forty-six…four times in one night!

"Shhh, shhh, shhh, it's okay my sweet boy. What's wrong with my sweet wittle boy?", I whispered as I reached over the white crib railing.

His diaper was flat in the front and there wasn't the stench of poop escaping from the back.

"A WAAA! WAAA!" I held his chest close to mine as I sat in the cushioned navy- blue rocker.

He wiggled and scooted himself until his head was right under my breast…seriously, Christian? I just nursed you at three-thirty!

I felt like a twenty-four- hour diner with one waitress, and one cook. I made the meals from scratch and served them… from my boobs.

My eyelids felt like miniature steel doors, but the thought of my nipples cracking and bleeding swung them wide open. I took a deep breath and positioned his head so that his nose lined up with my nipple…Thank goodness! He latched on like a pro!

Even with just two hours of sleep, I was restless. All I could think about was the big kids missing the bus and Ryan not getting his lunch if I overslept.

I could tell by the milk drooling from the corner of Christian's mouth that he was satisfied. Maybe I should try to put him down? - Nah, more than likely he would wake up screamin' and hollerin' like he hadn't eaten in ten days.

Maybe I can catch an hour before it's time to wake everyone up. I got comfortable in the rocker and started to doze off.

Home-Work

"Mommy! Mommy! I can't reach my cereal bowl! It's too high!", shouted Amaya. "

O, shoot! I overslept!

"Maya, go sit at the table and Mommy will be there in a minute," I told her.

Her hair was sticking up like she had just gotten off a roller coaster and the sleep crumbs on her face told me she hadn't washed her face yet.

I put Christian in his crib and sprinted across the hallway. I twisted the doorknob and yelled,

"Michael! RJ! Get up guys!" I snatched the covers away from their bodies to motivate them.

"Ah, man! I'm too tired to go to school today!", said RJ.

"My stomach *and* head hurt!", said Michael.

"Well, I told you all to turn the game off and go to bed. So, that's too bad! Everybody is going to school today!", I said as I walked towards the kitchen.

"What's wrong Maya Pooh?", I asked seeing her eyes blurred with tears.

"Mommy, I'm just sooo hungry! My tummy is gonna fall on the floor and, and then I'm gonna die! - It's not fair!", she said with tears falling from her big brown eyes.

"Awww, Maya! Mommy will make sure your tummy stays *inside* your body. Here's your cereal, Princess", I said while sitting the pink bowl of *Unicorn Puffs* on the floral placemat in front of her.

She sniffled and rubbed the tears away from her eyes with her little fingers.

"ANK-QU WOM-WE!, " she said with a mouth full of sugar-coated puffs.

"YOU'RE WELCOME MAYA!"

I speed away to the boys' room and peeked around the white door frame…they were still in bed!

"Seriously, boys?! You're going to miss the bus!"

I reached inside the "dungeon" where their nice shirts were half-hung, shoes thrown about on the floor, and clothes that were too small lapped over the top shelf.

"RJ, you put on the khaki shorts and the shark T-shirt and Michael you put on the blue cargo shorts with the baseball shirt," I said, flinging the clothes onto the bed like frisbees.

I dashed to Maya's room and grabbed a comb, brush, moisturizer, elastic tie, and her favorite cotton-candy pink bow.

141

Maya was still shoving cereal into her tiny mouth at the round kitchen table.

I dropped the "mini salon" on the chair next to Maya, splattered my hands with moisturizer, and guided the comb through the ends of her hair.

"OUCH MOMMY! IT HUUURRRTS!", screamed Maya.

I thought she would be too distracted with stuffing her face to notice me combing through her tangled coils.

"I know, I know. Mommy is almost done and it's going to look super pretty!", I reassured her.

"Oookayy," she said.

I smoothed her curls into a cute little puff that sat on the top of her head and clipped her favorite bow in the front.

"All done! Now, go brush your teeth and put your clothes on like a big girl for mommy...ok?"

"Yes, Mommy! I'm a big girl! I can do it!", she darted through the living room and down the hallway.

"Stop running Maya!", I yelled after her. A bump on the head was the last thing I needed this morning!

"Good morning Steph," Ryan said as he grabbed a coffee mug from the white wooden cabinet.

"Good morning Honey... sorry I didn't have your coffee and bagel ready for you this morning. Christian is draining me – literally!"

"It's fine Steph. I think this I.T. guy can figure out the coffee maker and toaster," Ryan said with a grin.

"I didn't pack your lunch either," I shook my head.

"That's ok Steph. I can grab something close to the office," Ryan said.

I raised up on my tippy toes and pecked him on the cheek - I hadn't brushed my teeth yet so a kiss on the lips was off limits.

The boys walked into the kitchen still looking half asleep. I slapped a piece of toast and cup of orange juice into each of their hands and ran to check on Maya.

She was fully dressed and admiring her pink bow in the full-length mirror behind her bedroom door. I glanced down at her feet. Her shoes made it seem like she was standing with her legs crossed. I quickly swapped her shoes around.

"BONK, BONKKK!"

"The bus is here!", I yelled out to the boys. I could hear them twisting the doorknob so, I ran out to give them hugs and I-love-yous.

As the boys ran towards the bus, I waved to Mr. Randy and he nodded. He wasn't the most social, but he was patient. One time, he waited on my boys for five whole minutes when RJ split his pants running to the bus.

It was only eight and I felt like I had put in a full day's work.

"Mommy, is it time for school?", Maya asked as she tugged on my heart covered robe.

"Almost Maya. Grab your backpack and wait for me right here," I said, pointing to the corner next to the front door.

143

Ryan was sitting at the kitchen table with burnt, half-eaten multigrain toast as he sipped coffee and scrolled through his phone. His two strands of gray peaked through his thick black hair.

"Hey, Ry -"

"Geez, Steph! I didn't see you standing there!", he said, nearly dropped his "World's Best Dad" mug.

"Sorry...you mind staying here while I take Maya to school? I *really* don't wanna wake Christian until I'm ready to feed him."

"I can stay- but only for about ten minutes. I need to leave by eight-twenty to get to the site on time."

"Ok", I said as I rushed towards the front door – no Maya.

"Amaya Rose Carter! It's time to go!"

Her curly puff bounced as she came prancing out of her room.

"I was, I was just looking at how pink and pretty my bow is!"

"Yes, it's very pink Sweetie. Let's go see Ms. Christy and your friends," I said closing the door behind us.

I could see Ryan pacing on the cobblestone walkway, with his hands in his pockets as soon as I pulled into the driveway...

Seriously, Ryan? You couldn't wait for me to get back in the house? What if Christian is crying his eyes out with no one in the house?

I yanked my purse out of the passenger seat and hustled

right pass Ryan to prevent myself from exploding.

I could hear his shoes grinding on the walkway as he spun around to investigate what he had done wrong – I didn't look back though.

I sat the baby monitor on the marbled bathroom counter and grabbed my toothbrush. I brushed, rinsed, and hopped into the shower. I inhaled and exhaled deeply as the massage spray setting relaxed my muscles.

This was the best part of the day, some time to myself… "MWAAA! MMWA! WA!"- Christian's up! I threw open the shower door and pulled my towel from the rack.

There was no point putting on a bra since I was popping my boobs out in a few minutes. I threw Ryan's old college T-shirt over my head and stepped into my high-waisted panties and black leggings. They hid my tiger stripes and saggy skin, so they were a regular part of my wardrobe.

"Good morning, Mommy's man! Let's put on fresh pampy and your cute little puppy dog onsie," I said trying to calm him.

His eyes were like full moons as he looked up at me, smiling. "Ahhh!", he cooed as a stream of baby pee splashed my cheek. At least it didn't land in my mouth like last time.

"All done!", I said tossing the diaper in the diaper pail.

"Let's get you something to eat little man!" I grabbed my phone, TV remote, and sat in the beige leather recliner with Christian propped on my shoulder.

I flipped the channel to *Cheaters Court* and started pressing on both breasts – trying to remember which side I nursed him on last. I lifted the bottom of my shirt over the left breast and breakfast was served!

Jessica wanted Austin to pay her three-thousand dollars and I don't blame her! Seventeen years? That's a looong time to pick up his nasty clothes and listen to him snore every night – *after* he snuck in from the other woman's house - Just trifling!

Just as Judge Jessie was about to read the verdict, *"Blrinnng! Blrinng!"*

"This is just a reminder that you have an appointment for, Christian Carter on March ninth, at ten o'clock a.m. Please press "1" to confirm or call to cancel."

"Mmcht!" I forgot this was tomorrow! I pressed "1" on the keypad anyway. I laid Christian on the blue and green bear shaped play gym. His face lit up as he gazed and reached for the dangling rattles and shapes.

The smell of mildew hit me in the face as soon as I opened the washing machine door. "Seriously, Stephanie?!" I could've sworn I put them in the dryer last night!

I started to retrace my thoughts...Now I remember! I was about to put these in the dryer when Maya reported ghosts were dancing in her closet.

When I was on my way back to the laundry room after playing Paranormal Police, I noticed a dirt road from the boys' room to the living room so, I started sweeping.

I lifted the laundry detergent from the shelf, "Ewww!" I plopped the container on the washer as I tried to shake the pain out of my wrist. I set the knob to "Quick Wash" and pressed "Start".

Working Late

"Hey Mom, where are the *Cheezy Bites*?", asked RJ, looking on the kitchen counter.

"They're still in the oven. Go get started on your homework and I'll bring them to you."

I grabbed the baby monitor and went to check on Maya. She was complaining of a tummy ache when I picked her up from school. She had fallen asleep in her bed with her arms wrapped around Star Dazzle, a plush unicorn that was bigger than her.

I gently pulled the door closed and headed back to the kitchen,

"Hey Mom, where are the Chee-"

"I'm getting them out now, RJ!"

RJ was going to send me to an early grave over freakin' *Cheezy Bites*! He always acted like he was literally starving when he came home from school.

Between his relentless snacking and Michael asking for seconds *every* night, our grocery bill looked like we were feeding an army. As soon as Christian gets his first set of pegs, he'll be joining his brothers in the Carter Food Eating Contest.

I had been cleaning all day, but the house was still a mess! I was too afraid to wake Christian and Maya so I decided to hold off on vacuuming.

"Mom, can we have more? I *only* ate three. RJ ate the rest," said Michael.

"Just grab something from the pantry – a bag of chips, crackers, or cookies," I replied.

WORK HARD PLAY HARDLY

"Can I get something from the pantry, too?", asked RJ.

"Both of you, get *one* thing from the pantry – that's it until dinner!"

I filled the stainless- steel sink with hot water and dish soap as they rummaged through the snack shelf of the pantry like city rats… Why did we always have so many dishes?

Maybe I should just get rid of all but one dish and one cup for each person and use plastic forks and spoons since they're pretty cheap.

"Seriously, Stephanie?!" I forgot to take the chicken breast out of the freezer! I can't get dinner started with frozen meat! I filled a huge mixing bowl with warm water and dumped the packet of chicken into it.

I couldn't even blame the boys this time. When I was working at the office, I'd sometimes tell one of them to take out something from the freezer…I missed going to work.

Staying at home was *definitely* saving us money. A top-notch daycare, one where they actually pay attention to your kid, costs close to seven-hundred dollars a month!

To add to that, we were saving by having Maya at pre-school part-time instead of full. I missed it though … I missed talking to adults, having a lunch break, or just driving home from work *without* kids in the car.

The big boys went to the park with Eric from next door and it was time to get Christian up from his nap. I hated waking a sleeping baby, but if I didn't, tonight would be a Hollerin' Hell.

I nursed Christian and put him in the oscillating swing.

"*Woosh! Click. Woosh! Click.*" Hopefully, I could pump five or so ounces before checking on Maya.

"Mommy, my tummy feels all better!", said Maya in her pink rhinestone tiara and bedazzled cape.

"Are you feeling better Sweetie?"

"Yes! Can I have juice? *Pleeeze!*"

"Grab a box of apple juice from the refrigerator door - be *careful.*

"Ok Mommy," she said as her blingy cape trailed behind her.

"*SMASH!*" "Oh no, oh no Mommy!" I make a BIG mess!

"Don't move Maya! Just like when you play freeze tag with Ella!"

I unhooked my boobs from the suction cups as quickly as I could. I sat the two ounces of liquid gold on the cherrywood end table, not noticing *Mini Molly's* tiny purple purse underneath -

Splash!

"Oooh, Shiiii-take mushrooms!!!" (I couldn't say what I really wanted to with Maya nearby) I could feel myself about to shed a stream of tears, but I held them in and went to rescue Maya.

There were chunks of glass and strawberry jam splattered over the tan kitchen tiles. Maya stood as still as a post with her face buried inside her pink superhero gloves.

"It's ok Maya. I know it was an accident," I lifted her over the mess and carried her to the kitchen chair.

"Sit here sweetie and Mommy will get your apple juice."

I handed her the green box of juice.

"Mommy, I tried to get my juice and everything just break!"

"I know, I know...", I said while tossing the big chunks of glass into the garbage.

I grabbed the broom for what seemed like the hundredth time today, and an old towel from the laundry room. I poured hot water and sprayed *Super Clean n' Shine* on the jam stains.

"*Bee-beep!*" Ryan opened the front door. The house was a mess and I hadn't even started dinner yet! I left Maya and the mess to greet Ryan.

I caught a glimpse of my messy hair and sweat-stained face in the mirror hanging in the hallway. I looked like a mechanic who worked on an old Buick from sun-up to sun- down. I'd be lucky if Ryan didn't serve me with divorce papers after seeing his house *and* wife look mess!

"Hi honey! How was your day?", I asked, trying to lighten the mood before he saw the wreckage of Hurricane Carter.

"It was good – nothing special, but good – What in the atomic bomb happened here today?!

I could see his eyes scanning over the tiny pieces of trash on the area rug, the plate of crumbs on the study table and, the two ounces of liquid gold dripping over the edge of the table.

I knew it was a mess, but it's something about watching someone else look at the mess you're responsible for – it looks ten times worse.

"It's just been a crazy day – Maya had a tummy-ache, the

boys eat everything and -"

"There's my little man!", he said reaching down toward the baby swing.

"Where's Maya and the boys?"

"Maya is sitting in front of a pile of jam, drinking apple juice and the boys are playing ball with Eric."

Ryan made me feel like the house was a bad daycare. One where you pick your kid up in a loaded diaper, the floor is covered in dirt and snack time crumbs, and the teacher doesn't have a good answer for why your kid has on some other kid's pants.

I finished cleaning the mess in the kitchen while Maya and Christian sat in Ryan's lap. It was dinner time and all I had was a bowl of half-thawed chicken, spilled breast milk, and jam- stained leggings.

Work Day

"Hi Ms. Nelson. Could you make sure Ryan gets this?", I asked, raising the camouflage bookbag over the counter.

Why was it so heavy? Better yet, why did it look like he had been battling in the trenches of a warzone? – I was beyond embarrassed.

"Sure Mrs. Carter. I'll buzz Mrs. Johansen to send him up," she said.

"Thank you so much," I responded, as I hoisted the car seat from the floor to the front of my leggings.

I lugged the car seat to the drop -off circle and secured it onto the base. Surprisingly, Christian appeared to be unbothered

WORK HARD PLAY HARDLY

by the inconvenient detour.

I hated rushing, but how could I avoid it when my middle son forgets *everything* – expect his lunch?! We were right to name him after his dad – neither one of them can remember a thing!

He's always saying, "Oh, that's today?" or something like, "I thought you were going to do that" or my all-time favorite "Well, you know I work full-time so, it's easier if you do it."

I guess being a stay-at-home-mom is a day at *Serenity Spa.* Where I prop my feet up and Maya comes to massage them, Christian brings *me* some milk, and the boys serve *me Cheezy Bites!* – he clearly has no idea what it's like taking care of the Carter Crew, him included!

I threw the elephant diaper bag on my shoulder and released the car seat from the base. I signed us in with a minute to spare. I thumbed through the *Moms Club* magazine and all of a sudden, my wrists and shoulders were aching - my knees and ankles, too.

My joints hurt from time to time – but that comes with the territory. I'm thirty-nine with a three-month-old (what was me and my uterus thinking), a three-year-old, and a ten and twelve- year-old – pain, mental and physical, is expected.

I had never seen my wrists as red as beets or my ankles look like jet-puffed marshmallows.

"Christian's growth is above the curve for his age," said Dr. Adams as he traced the chart with his finger. I didn't expect anything less, being that he has an in-home milk factory and all.

"That's great Dr. Adams…how long do you think I should

breastfeed him? – especially since he's growing so fast?"

"Even though he's growing above the average, the APA recommends until he is a year old and no table food until six months."

(Seriously, Dr. Adams? You want my body to produce milk for a future linebacker - for a full year?")

"Ok, I'll keep it going!"

"Ok Mrs. Carter, we'll see Christian back for his six - month check-up – both of you keep up the good work!"

I strapped the eighteen-and-a-half-pound little turkey into his car seat. I didn't want Christian becoming a victim of the hacking coughs and snotty noses in the office just to schedule a check-up, so we headed straight for the exit.

I caught a glimpse of my reflection in the sun visor mirror before backing out of the parking lot. YIKES! I know my biracial skin doesn't exactly love the sun's rays, but I had *never* had sunburn spreading across the bridge of my nose, from cheek to cheek. - I should stop skipping the sunscreen.

My body is so tired – so tired I thought about pulling onto the side of the road. But if someone kidnapped us, that would definitely put me behind schedule.

I only had about an hour before scooping Maya from the Little Scholars Academy and Christian needed lunch – come to think of it, I hadn't eaten anything at all.

I dropped the armful of mail onto the granite countertop, washed my hands and got ready to nurse Christian – he was sound asleep -Yes!

I can *finally* have a moment in the bathroom without a baby crying in the next room or Maya standing on the other side of the door asking, "Mommy, are you pooping for a *long* time?"

I grabbed some of the mail from the counter and took my seat on the throne. I really should shave more often – my legs felt like cacti in the Sahara and my ankles were retaining water like they did when I was pregnant.

Bright Star Health? – we haven't had any medical bills since Christian was born. I tore through the white envelope- 'Mrs. Carter, it's that time of year again blah, blah'- I freakin' forgot about this!

The health insurance through Ryan's work *makes* us take bloodwork every year– supposedly for *prevention.* It was prevention alright – it was preventing me from having one moment of sanity in this house. I could just not go, but our premium would go up. We couldn't afford that with boys that eat like wild stallions!

"WAAAA! WA -WAAAA! So much for my "mini staycation" – it's lunch time!

Lunches packed…check. Dinner served…check. Laundry folded…check, and Maya was in bed without seeing or hearing dancing ghosts – I was knocking it out of the park!

"Mom, there's this thing-", It was never good when RJ started a sentence with that phrase.

"What thing?", I asked in terror.

"Well, Mrs. Johansen…today she said that we all have to do the science fair at school… I thought I didn't have to do it."

"When is it due?", I was more terrified than ever.

"It's due on tomorrow, but I-"

"Seriously, RJ?!! Are you being serious right now?", I shouted.

"I already know what I'm going to do though."

"And that is -?"

"Well, my hypothesis is, 'Playing video games before you go to bed, helps you sleep better'," he answered.

"And how have you tested this hypothesis?"

"This week, me and Michael have been playing the game right before we go to bed and guess what?"

"What RJ?"

"We oversleep the next morning after we play the game – it helps us sleep better!"

"You know what RJ -", I was about three milliseconds from strangling him, "You all have been studying volcanoes, let's just do something with that."

"Ok," he said, shrugging his bony shoulders.

My joints were aching and I was as tired as a bear in hibernation – but Big Ryan was on a strict sleep schedule (since he was the *only* one that had to work) so, it was all on me to figure this out.

When I finally do get to bed, the snoring coming from Ryan is going to sound like an old lawn mower cutting ten-inch-high grass.

So, me and my aching body would end up on the couch…well, until Christian was ready to eat at the late-night diner… it was going to be a long night.

Worked Out

I could feel the heaviness of Christian's diaper on my forearm as we stood on the front lawn.

"Hi Mr. Bill!', I waved like a kid in a parade, "How's Mrs. Nancy?"

"Still on my back about the cigarettes – and bossing me around," Mr. Bill chuckled.

"Well, you know what they say, 'Happy wife, happy life!'", I reminded him.

"Well, *I* always say, "Be like Bill, sit back, and chill!"

"That's a good one Mr. Bill!"

"This little fella of yours is getting bigger by the day!", he said as he handed me a handful of envelopes.

"I'll tell Nancy you asked about her - see ya' tomorrow Mrs. Stephanie!" he smiled and waved as he drove away in the mail truck.

I think it's safe to say that my mailman is my BFF these days. Since I traded in my favorite burgundy skirt suit for black leggings and an oversized T-shirt, my interactions with adults were at a minimum.

On some days, when he wasn't' too busy, Ryan would call to check-in with generic questions about how my day was going (which were mostly Christian-based questions) or to make a dinner request for the night. Those phone calls lasted about ten minutes at the most so, I looked forward to my conversations with Mr. Bill.

I enjoy spending time with the kids, but I missed talking about my kids to people who aren't kids themselves- or just talking about grown-up TV shows with actual grown-ups.

Christian swung peacefully as the mobile with zoo animals spun over his head. I plopped down on the sofa to sort the mail. Blue Star? – that was quick.

These results ought to be worth pure gold for all I had to go through to get them. The girl drawing blood must have been fresh out of school or not have gone to school at all. She dug around my poor little arm three times only to end up drawing blood from my hand – I still have sore spots!

I didn't know much about reading these numbers, but I could see that several things were printed in red, which meant something was out of whack. I got Nurse Cheryl on the phone.

"Stephanie, you must've read my mind! Dr. Stevens wanted me to schedule a telemedicine appointment about your labs – do you have time to do it now?"

"Yes, that's exactly why I was calling – what does all this mean?

"Hi Stephanie. This is Dr. Stevens. The ANA profile on your labs came back positive. I'm not sure why the insurance ordered this - maybe your family history, but this profile tells us if there's a possibility for autoimmune diseases -"

"Like what kind of diseases?", I interrupted.

"Like lupus, multiple sclerosis, and other diseases where the immune system is attacking the body… Have you had any pain in your joints, skin rashes of any kind, or feeling tired?

"Come to think of it, I noticed a rash across my face about a week ago - I thought it was a reaction to the sun. My joints ache and swell and I'm tired all the time, but I have four kids – "

"Based on your symptoms and the lab report, it sounds like you've been experiencing lupus flare-ups. I am going to send your chart to Dr. Iman, a rheumatologist, for further testing."

"Thank you, Dr. Stevens", I said before ending the call.

I rushed to the internet to find out all I could about lupus – this looked and sounded just like me. My hair had been falling out, too. I thought it was my hormones trying to straighten out from being pregnant.

I had only heard of lupus once in my life and I didn't know it was a disease that stayed with you forever – and to think, all this time I've been dealing with this just thinking I'm a tired stay-at-home-mom.

Life at the Carter's was about to be redefined! I couldn't carry the load of the household alone. If I was going to live with lupus, I needed my boys and Ryan to start helping me out around here. This isn't just *my* house, this is *our* home.

15 The Selfless Woman

She would give you the shirt off her back, even it meant that she would get eaten alive by a swarm of mosquitoes. She can't bear the thought of the people she loves going lacking or wanting for anything. The Selfless Woman will always do what is best for the greater good, even when she feels alone and ignored.

"Me-Time", a good night's sleep, or eating an actual meal with a fork are often foreign events to the Selfless Woman. She whizzes around like she is powered by *Duracell* and is usually doing three or more things at the same time.

She's often involved in various organizations. She's presiding over the PTA on Tuesday nights, leading choir rehearsal on Thursday night, and the team leader on the big marketing project Monday through Friday and sometimes for a few hours on Saturday.

Getting the Selfless Woman to do something for herself can feel like pulling teeth. Often times, she will cash in all of her time doing something for someone else. She doesn't mind giving herself away, but there are days that she wishes she saw the Cape of Sacrifice on someone else's shoulders. There are days that she needs someone to give themselves up to what she needs and wants.

The people in her life have become so accustomed to her giving away everything she has that they become certified takers. A certified taker will accept whatever you are willing to give and God forbid if you can't give what they're asking for, they'll get upset! In most cases, the Selfless Woman has no limits or boundaries when it comes to giving her all and last and takers are well aware of that.

By definition, the Selfless Woman is concerned with the needs and wishes of others more than her own. The selflessness of The Selfless Woman creates a barrier when it comes to her taking care of herself -Stephanie is no exception.

The Healthy Truth About Stephanie

When people think of a Stay-at-home-mom (SAHM), they picture this woman eating her favorite snacks on the couch while talking to other SAHMs about how they can't stand Valerie on *All the Days of Our Lives*. While she's doing this, her well-behaved children are taking a nap or quietly painting a Picasso in the next room – Negative!

From my experience, being a SAHM can drain the natural life out of you! Stephanie, being the selfless person that she is, decided to leave her job to help with the financial burden of childcare. She was available to her family's needs and wants 24/7 as a chauffeur, private chef, cleaning service, nanny, and nurse.

WOMAN TAKE OFF YOUR CAPE

Stephanie made sure that her husband and children had everything that they needed and most of the things that they wanted.

To add to her acts of selflessness, Stephanie made the decision to breastfeed her son. Breastfeeding can be emotionally and physically taxing for moms, especially when they have other children to take care of. Stephanie spent most of her day under a tight schedule of drop-offs, pick-ups, clean-ups, and appointments.

On most days, she barely ate a decent meal and showered just long enough to get minimally clean. Stephanie's health was fading before her eyes, but her focus on what her family wanted and needed allowed the signs and symptoms of lupus to go unnoticed.

Lupus, also known as systemic lupus erythematosus (SLE), is a long-term condition in which the immune system attacks the body. Anytime the immune system attacks the body rather than protect it, this is an autoimmune disease. Guess who has the most autoimmune diseases in America? – Women! One in every six Americans have an autoimmune disease and women make up 78 percent those cases (10) !

One would think that since autoimmune diseases are a major health issue for women that we would be well-versed on the signs and symptoms. In reality, our long, flowing capes help us to disguise how we feel and since there or over 80 autoimmune diseases, a misdiagnosis is not uncommon.

African – American woman are the most likely group of women to have lupus. They are three times more likely to have lupus than Caucasian women. Lupus causes more complications and a higher rate of death among African – American women. Hispanic, Asian, Native American, and Alaskan native women are more likely to have lupus than Caucasian women (11).

Lupus can affect the entire body, causing a host of signs and symptoms that cape-wearing women may overlook. Signs and symptoms may include:

Rash on the cheeks and the nose (butterfly, malar rash)

Pain or swelling in the hands, feet, around the eyes or other joints

Sores in the mouth or nose

Feeling extreme fatigue

Headaches

Radiation to the chest

Sensitivity to sunlight or fluorescent light

Low-grade fevers

Chest pain when taking a deep breath

Hair loss

Fingers and/or toes turn white or blue from stress or cold (Raynaud's Disease)

Your doctor will not be able to diagnose you with lupus based on signs and symptoms alone. Other testing is needed because lupus symptoms can look like other diseases, your symptoms can come and go, or you may have a different set of symptoms than you did a few months ago.

An antibody blood test, most likely the ANA test will be done. The test is not a specific test for lupus, but ninety-seven percent of people with lupus have a positive ANA test. Urine tests and tissue biopsies can give your doctor more insight and assist them in making a diagnosis (12).

Getting a diagnosis for any autoimmune disease can be a long road. Remember, that you are doing the best thing for your health and well-being. You deserve to have the tools and information you need to live your healthiest life, even with lupus.

16 Take a Selfie!

When you are selfless by nature, the word "selfish" is enough to make you itch! What does it *really* mean to be selfish? To be selfish means that you put your needs and wishes above the needs and wishes of others. When we think about someone being selfish, we think of a permanent way of being. How would you feel about being selfish every Thursday night from the hours of six o'clock to eight o'clock?

When you think of being selfish for a temporary period of time, it doesn't seem so evil does it? As a woman, temporary selfishness is needed! Temporary selfishness is what gives you permission to have a girls' not out, relax and read a book alone, or take a long soak in the bathtub without feeling guilty about it.

I like to refer to this temporary period of selfishness as "Taking a Selfie". When you take a selfie with your phone, you're trying to find the best lighting, pose, and filters that make YOU look like you just stepped off the runway! "Taking a Selfie" in your life has exactly the same concept!

Pick out the day and time that you want to "Take a Selfie" and put it on your schedule. Let your husband, friends, family, and kids, big and little, know that you will *not* be available to them on Selfie Saturday (or Monday or whichever day you choose).

You may feel like it's impossible to plan a few hours that are just for you, someone won't understand. Well, guess what? They'll learn and they'll like it! They will all notice that you are happier, healthier, and more attentive to them (when you're not taking a selfie), so it's a win-win! When you've planned time for decompression and rejuvenation, managing the day-to-day becomes a bit easier.

Still not sold on your circle embracing Selfie Saturday? Two hours of being "selfish" every week leaves you with one hundred, sixty-six hours to carry out all of your selfless acts. Look at it this way, people usually respect the selfishness of selfish people - they cater to what they want or stay away from them altogether! So, going to your new routine will train your crew to respect your Selfie Day just the same!

If you don't balance your selflessness with temporary selfishness, you put yourself at risk for physical and mental burn out, disappointment, and clinical depression. Stop waiting for someone to put on your cape and relieve you or your duties as The Selfless Woman - it's not going to happen.

It's important to pour time, attention, and affection into yourself. Your well will run dry waiting for others to do for you what you have the power and ability to do for yourself. Remember, you teach others how to treat you!

If they never see you taking care of yourself or being thoughtful towards yourself, it's likely that they won't treat you in that way either. Once they see you treating yourself well, they will follow your lead.

166

17 It's Time To Save YOU!

If you've read this far, I hope that that you now have a clearer picture of how cape-wearing has stolen the life of health and peace that you deserve. I hope that as you walked through the journeys of these five women, that you could see the pitfalls of your own journey. Sandra, Andrea, Erica, Michelle, and Stephanie, represent so many women who are battling the weight of the cape.

You may be wondering, "Is it possible for me to save the day for someone else and save myself?" The answer is, Yes! As I mentioned in the beginning of this book, the cape is not an everyday accessory. Putting on the cape every day, for every person that calls and every situation you face is like putting on a ball gown to go to work – it's just too much! I wouldn't say that the cape is for special occasions only, but you should only wear it as needed.

Who decides when it's needed? You do! Just because someone is requesting you to play the superhero doesn't mean you have to. Reserve wearing the cape for when it really counts. Wearing the cape counts when you can present yourself to

your family, community, and yourself as a whole woman, one that is taking care of herself, mind, body, and spirit.

Remember that taking off the cape is a process, but the reward is well worth it. You won't be perfect (remember, we talked about that earlier). You'll still have days, weeks, maybe even months that you find yourself going back into your old habits. The good thing about books is that you can always re-read them! Go to your journal, your place of prayer, and meditation to hit the reset button.

You can truly show up for others when you learn to fly for yourself first! I hope that these tools empower you to experience a life that is abundant in peace, mental clarity, and physical well-being. Woman, you can take off your cape and start saving YOU!

ACKNOWLEDGMENTS

I give thanks to you, God, for entrusting me with the vision to write such an empowering message that will impact women all over the world. I thank you for sending me a message regarding the health and well-being of women, through my own tests, trials, and failures. You always make a way.

I am grateful for you, my loving husband James. You have supported my vision in composing this work. Not only have you supported this work, but you've always supported my dreams and have never doubted my ambitions. Thank you for your sacrifice and for carrying my load when it gets too heavy. I love you.

I am thankful for you, my children, Cadence and Macklen. You two are a great inspiration for why I pursue big dreams. I know that you, too will dream big. Thank you for giving your Mama a few quiet hours to write this book. I love you.

I am blessed to have my parents, Marvin and Teresa. Thank you for instilling in me that anything is possible through faith in God and hard work. Thank you for your prayers and supporting me from the beginning of time. I love you.

I am thankful to my brothers, Montrez and Marcus and my God-sister Nydia. You have believed in me and supported my efforts throughout the years. Thanks for making me feel that I'm the smartest person you know. I love you.

I am thankful for my Mt. Zion CME Church family. Thank you for your prayers and unwavering support for so many years. I love you.

I am thankful my grandmother Annie, godmother Sandra, my friends, and all the women who have said an encouraging word or have lifted me in prayer. Thank you for believing in me. I love you.

About The Author

Dr. Candace McMillon-Dantley is a passionate health and wellness empowerment speaker and writer, a licensed chiropractor, and a women's health program coordinator. For six years, she served her community as Gadsden County's first African American female chiropractor.

For the past seven years, she has educated her community and church during a monthly health awareness initiative. Her love for writing and creating ignited the launch of *The Doc Knows*, a women's health empowerment website.

She is a wife and mother of two who enjoys family game night, picnics, and movie night with her family. When she's not spending time with her family, she is doing a new workout or creating healthy recipes for her family.

As a native of Gadsden County, she has always had a heart to serve her community through health awareness and education. It is her dream that men and women of all backgrounds have access to quality health services and are empowered through health education.

See More From Dr. Candace at...

www.thedocknows.com

@drcandace
@thedocknowsomenshealth

The Doc Knows

Notes

1. Council, Women's Business Enterprise National. WBENC News. *Behind the Numbers: The State of Women-Owned Businesses in 2018.* [Online] October 10, 2018. https://www.wbenc.org/blog-posts/2018/10/10/behind-the-numbers-the-state-of-women-owned-businesses-in-2018.

2. About Adult BMI. *Centers for Disease Control.* [Online] August 29, 2017. https://www.cdc.gov/healthyweight/assessing/bmi/adult_bmi/index.html.

3. American Heart Association Diet and Lifestye Recommendations. *American Heart Association.* [Online] August 15, 2015. https://www.heart.org/en/healthy-living/healthy-eating/eat-smart/nutrition-basics/aha-diet-and-lifestyle-recommendations.

4. Services, Administration Substance Abuse and Mental Health. *Key substance use and mental health indicators in the United States.* Rockville, MD:enter for Behavioral Health Statistics and Quality, Substance Abuse and Mental Health Services Administration : Results from the 2018 National Survey on Drug Use and Health (HHS Publication No. PEP19-5068, NSDUH Series H-54), 2019.

5. Depression. *National Institute of Mental Health.* [Online] February 2018. https://www.nimh.nih.gov/health/topics/depression/index.shtml#part_145396.

6. Mental Health. *World Health Organization* . [Online] April 17, 2018. https://www.who.int/mental_health/prevention/suicide/suicideprevent/en/
.

7. Marcia Boraas, MD, FACS and Sameer Gupta, MD, MPH. Breast Self-Exam. *BreastCancer.Org.* [Online] October 24, 2019. https://www.breastcancer.org/symptoms/testing/types/self_exam.

8. Hereditary Breast and Ovarian Cancer. *Centers For Disease Control and Prevention.* [Online] March 25, 2020. https://www.cdc.gov/genomics/disease/breast_ovarian_cancer/risk_categ ories.htm.

9. McMillon-Dantley, Dr. Candace. A Rite of Passage to Womanhood or Endometriosis? *The Doc Knows.* [Online] May 10, 2019. https://www.thedocknows.com/post/a-rite-of-passage-to-womanhood-or-endometriosis.

10. *Sex Differences in Autoimmune Disease from a Pathological Perspective.* DeLisa Fairweather, Sylvia Frisancho-Kiss, Noel R. Rose. 2008, The American Journal of Pathology, pp. 600-609.

11. Lupus and Women. *Office of Women's Health.* [Online] March 25, 2019. https://www.womenshealth.gov/lupus/lupus-and-women#12.

12. Lab Tests For Lupus. *Lupus Foundaiton of America.* [Online] July 15, 2013. https://www.lupus.org/resources/lab-tests-for-lupus.

Made in the USA
Las Vegas, NV
12 February 2022

43774748R00105